The Moody Pews

The Moody Pews

A 52 Week Devotional for the Flower Child / Baby Boomer

Sandra L. Brown, M.A.

Tsaba House
Reedley, California

Cover design by Bookwrights Design
Interior Design and typography by Pete Masterson, Aeonix Publishing Group
Senior Editor, Jodie Nazaroff

"I am Sam, Sam I am" used with permission from Dr. Seuss Enterprises, L.P.
McDonald's Trademark used with permission from McDonalds Corporation.
Cover photos: courtesy Andrea Schwagerl; "girl with signs" and "granny glasses"
courtesy of Annie's Photography; "rock band" courtesy Photodisc.
All scripture quotations, unless otherwise noted, are taken from the *King James Version* of the Bible.

Library of Congress Cataloging-in-Publication Data

Brown, Sandra L., 1957-
    The moody pews : a 52 week devotional for the flower child-baby boomer / Sandra L. Brown.
      p. cm.
   ISBN 0-9725486-6-1 (pbk. : alk. paper)
   1. Baby boom generation--Religious life. 2. Devotional calendars. I. Title.
   BV4579.5.B76 2005
   242'.2--dc22

                        2004027675

Published by:
Tsaba House
2252 12th Street
Reedley, California 93654
Visit our website at: www.TsabaHouse.com

Printed in the United States of America

Contents

Contents

Contents

Acknowledgements

I wish to thank the Lord for being so much fun to work with! He's got a great sense of humor and it's been a blast to simply write the metaphors and stories as He gives them to me.

I thank all the people who are mentioned in the book for being enough of a part of my life that they surfaced as a metaphor for you to enjoy. I thank my husband Ken, whose Freudian Slips keep me writing continuously; and daughters Lindsay and Lauren, for their ever-amusing development that gives me plenty to write about. And to all my pets who stimulate metaphors by simply being them (Molly, Timber, Gabriel and Sophia).

And to many friends who have prayed for this project (Toni, Kathie, Margaret, Gail, Darlene, Sue, Leslie, and Scotta), and to my Mom who is an on-going resource of encouragement.

A big thanks for the ever creative mind of Pastor Randy Evans, brother in Rock and Roll (and the Lord), who came up with the title "The Moody Pews." Randy has been a good friend for 14 years, and counting, who shares a wild and wooly sense of humor!

A BIG (or my favorite word Gargantuan) THANK-YOU-OH-MY-GOSH-I-OWE-YOU-BIG-TIME to Monty and Michelle Nickerson who relentlessly researched the "legal-smegals" of copyright law for me! I couldn't have stayed motivated to complete this without your information! You guys are the best!

To my friend and previous boss, Scotta Orr who was my sounding board for these ridiculous essays and who encouraged me as to their value. She read enthusiastically as I submitted and resubmitted story after story. Thanks to my friend, Kathie Erwin, who kicked my butt to get me going on this project, which, as a fellow author, she has the right to do!

Also to any poor pastor that has tried to do something with me in my spirituality…I apologize for all the difficulties I **know** you endured. I hope you will see that it was not all in vain. I did finally **get it!** Special hugs to my favorite pastor-team Phil and Sue Engelman, who do an unbelievable job with weird baby boomers.

Last and never least are the publishers and editors at Tsaba House Publishing: Pam Schwagerl and Jodie Nazaroff. I am grateful that you grasped the sense of humor in our condition as baby boomers and saw it worthy of telling to our generation.

I end with a quote from Katie Kollwitz that describes my gratitude to the Lord for my gift of writing. She states, "I do not want to die until I have faithfully made the most of my talent and cultivated the seed that was placed in me until the last small twig has grown."

This book is dedicated to my nephew, Kyle Brown, a beautiful man with a charismatic personality, who died during the writing of this book. Kyle, you will be greatly missed but that fabulous smile will always be remembered.

Introduction

The Moody Pews is a reflection of the majority of "us" who now line the pews of the modern church. That "us" is 4.2 million people. For the most part, we are Boomers, X-ers and Y-ers who have walked an unusual path to the front doors of a church. We are noteworthy. We represent the largest subgroup within the Body of Christ. We bring to the pew issues not seen in recent eras. Not all of these are positive. In fact, we have changed the way ministers, in large part, do what they do because of who we are, and who we are not.

We challenge the concept of conventional "ministry" by bringing with us a myopic worldview that has been tainted by wild eras gone by. Boomers challenge the issue of discipleship (growing into Christlikeness) by what we have considered to now be "normal" in our lives: a national trend of 50% divorce rate, personal debt that exceeds yearly income, moving every five years, the lowest volunteer rate in 50 years, an apathetic detachment to issues that involve deep sacrifice, and a social hang over from all the clichés of the 60's/70's/80's that began with the concept "if it feels good, do it." Ministers must take what we bring to the pew and find some way (?!) of molding us into Christ-likeness. This is not an easy undertaking and because of that, and because of who we are and who we are not, the modern day church has been changing. Savvy marketing plans which aren't "too demanding" or don't use overly "religious words" that will scare us away are drawn up to attract us. "Seeker friendly" services target our populations with a "gentler" message. Discipleship, sacrifice, discipline and repentance are all words that are re-vocabularized for our emotional safety. This in itself is a benchmark within the history of the church. We have been coddled and spoon-fed theology in a way that has never been seen before in the church. Why?

Boomers, X-ers, and Y-ers have come from a different place to arrive in the pew. Our experiences, and thus worldview, are different than those from the people in the 1940's and 50's. Even as adults we still think, relate, and worship differently. We are still hard to reach. We are still socially narcissistic and want our theology soft so that it does not push too hard on our mantra, "Go with the flow." We want the flow, but only if it's going in our direction.

As adults of various ages, we straddle worlds—one foot is still in our memories of the good ol' days of rock and roll, and one is in the respectability of the church. Carefree and footloose we were and are, as we remember the physically, socially, and sexually turbulent times of the 60's/70's/80's. We still remember those times and more importantly, we still relate today through the worldview that was established in us as we grew up believing Joplin, Hendrix, or more recent rock and roll heroes of the 1980's. Society cannot over look that about us. Our decisions, choices and even our spirituality has been touched by incredibly marring eras. We are a generation that bears the imprint of that period of time in history. We carry that imprint to church and try to connect with a God we didn't even know when Woodstock was around. Church tries to speak to us at a level that we don't always relate to. Where are the metaphors for what we lived through? How is God relevant for me after the 60's/70's/80's? We straddle worlds...

Our generation often sits disgruntled in a pew feeling like we "ought" to be there but wondering if we are finding anything that relates to where we have been and how we got to the pew in the first place. Who addresses the mindset we have lived with all these years — the mindset that was formed by Martin Luther King Jr., peace marches, sit-ins, or the Kent State riots? Who talks about how The Beatles changed normal nerdy kids into freewheeling and free-lovin' hippies? Or the "Age of Aquarius" that spawned the "living together" tradition that the U.S.

has never recovered from? Yes, some minister can label it all "sin" and be done with it — labeling it in black and white terms that makes us feel misunderstood and unrelated to. We are the "hellions" the older ministers referred to. Ok, so we are. But we're in this pew and we're asking to be fed. So feed us something.

I hope in some small way this book will feed some of the hunger we all carry with us. I hope it touches us in places that we remember deeply, fondly, and longingly...memories that led us through odd places to finally get us in a pew. The Body of Christ is roomy and large enough for all of us. There is a place for you here, with your worldview and all that you brought with you. There is a place for you to remember and use what you lived through to grow into a stronger image of Christ. There is a place for The Rolling Stones and The Carpenters, for Led Zepplin and ZZ Top. It's all good stuff that the Lord can use to teach you about Him. Believe it or not, it's all clay in The Potter's Hand. Journey on...

Our Christian Walk

This is where it all begins, so the genesis is worth paying attention to. It might well serve as a mile marker in your life to tell you how you're doing and where you're headed; but to realistically appraise it, we have to step back to see it. We have to see it through other people's eyes. We might even have to ask others how they see our lives, or if they see Jesus in our lives. It might even hurt to hear the answer.

We can't be the only ones looking at our walk. If we are, it is like trying to see ourselves walk in a mirror. We can back up and walk toward the mirror, but we are only seeing the first few strides. We all look pretty good in the beginning, but St. Paul reminds us that it's how we finish the course that counts. And since most of us are only mid-way into this marathon, someone that's been watching should tell us how we're doing.

A sobering thought is that our lives are the only Bible some will ever read. What is it saying? This is a strong cup of coffee to a mind drunk on its own indulgences. Don't forget what our culture taught us: If it feels good, do it, Live and let live, Go with the flow. These aren't the building blocks of strong character. So we must be aware that we bring to this whole Christian experience, a mindset that was formational in how we got where we are. And whether we are aware of it or not, it has been instrumental in where we are today and how we are doing this "walk" thing. We all lived through something to be where we are and who we are. It is part of the tapestry that makes up the picture of our lives. Our lives are our walk. They are not separate. Even if it was a drunken, reefer-bleary walk to the altar to meet Christ, it was still part of the walk.

The essays and work sheets that follow take a look at our walk; or what I refer to as "my life dance." It helps us to set goals about where we want to get to. As you remember, "If you aim at nothing (don't have a goal), you will hit it every time." It helps us look at what is really happening in our lives; not what we wish was happening. It helps us get straight.

Turn the pages to the trippier parts of your life.

Dancing and Grooving
On This Earth for a Short While

I love Cat Stevens and have since the 70's. I find Cat to be an occasional source of spiritual inspiration. In Cat's song, "Oh Very Young," he reminds us that we are only on the earth a short period of time. As I listened to this song, I thought, *I guess that's one way of looking at it—we're dancing on this earth.* I tried to picture my life as a dance. It wasn't a pretty sight. I flashed to Miss Piggy in a tutu stumbling across the stage of life. Yep, that's been my dance!

In real life, I'm not a good dancer. My big debut comes to mind. In high school I was a dancer in our production of West Side Story. As you will remember, it was pretty rigorous stuff. Now try doing it in stiletto heels with slippery grease paint on your arms. During the dress rehearsal my puny dance partner's hands slipped off my grease painted arms. He was supposed to fling me wildly outward and then pull me back into him. I landed in the cello player's lap in the orchestra pit. But that was only *after* I wiped out the whole brass section. Later, during the actual performance, as I did a high kick over my head my deadly stiletto heel shot into the audience; and I'm sure, struck someone with the force of an arrow. I also remember at other times falling off the dance floor at discos, while trying to dance in platform shoes. Nope, I'm not a dancer.

Well, the fall into the orchestra pit and off the disco floor hasn't been my only left-footed stumble in this "dance of life." I tried to picture God looking at my life like a dance. He was in the audience with His playbill in hand and was cringing and covering His eyes at my wobbly waltzes, tripsy tangos, dippy discos and limping line dances. "No,

Sandy, start out with your right foot! Feel the rhythm, move with it not against it" He says, trying to choreograph this absurdity.

I'm Lucy Ricardo and Ethel Mertz trying to do a Latino dance to Ricky's snappy music. They have to pull me in with the hook they use for talent show rejects. That is how I feel when I look at my life as a dance; stumbles, full plunges into the orchestra pit, starting off with the wrong foot, being out of step with the rhythm, and losing my shoe and having to limp through the rest of the performance (i.e., life). My "life dance" looks more like I forgot to practice, missed all the rehearsals and just showed up for the performance. *"I hope that's not what God really sees,"* I think to myself.

To help me through this embarrassment, I tried to remember a time I actually danced "well". I just got more weird memories. The dances of the 70's didn't lend themselves to memories of dignity: the bump (!?), the funky chicken (!?), the "do-your-own-thing-cuz-no one-knows-what-you're-doing (!?), the jerk (!?), the grind (!?) Oh, please! There was no relief in those memories!

Maybe God really did look at our lives as a dance. Maybe He was looking for the flow; the synchronicity of a life lived in the divine tempo of His rhythm, the simplicity of the effort, the beauty...I began to think that at the White Throne Judgment it would just be easier to fast-forward the video to all my sin than to look at this issue of life as a dance. I think the aerial view of my life dance would look mighty ridiculous.

I remembered watching the beauty and the worship of sacred dancers before in a church service. Their movements were ones of grace, praise and poetic worship. I couldn't help but think that THAT was the "dance of life" God was looking for. Mine fell grossly short. The rhythm of my "life dance" had been punctuated with all the blunders of a novice struggling to make a piece of art out of stiletto heels. I didn't see my life as a progression of choreography, the dance steps of life taught by The King of Graceful Dancing who knew the amateur-ness of His beginning dancer. I didn't see the stumbles and sprained ankles as the inevitability of learning how to "dance on this earth for a short while."

Like everyone else, I wanted my dance to be perfect the first time. I wanted the beauty without the effort, the art without the failures.

Then, in the sweet way that only the Holy Spirit can promote, a whole new flood of imagery appeared. I remembered my children's plays and attempts at dancing when they were young. I was in the audience with a playbill in my hand. I was sitting up really straight so not to miss a thing. Ken was busy fighting all the other dads for the prime video spot to tape every little blunder my cuties would make. There were years they were singing snowflakes, dancing reindeers, or a lamb in a church play. My heart beat wildly as I mouthed their lines along with them; or as I held my breath as they twirled around on stage. I saw every little scrunch of their eyes, as they giggled, every little wiggle as they hated their costumes, every whisper as they talked to others on stage. I was proud of them for their attempts, and of course, as a proud parent I only saw their talent. We reassured them after performances that they did well. They always thought they should have done this or that differently. We saw the creativity of their "life dance" in a tight bud risking to blossom. And we always said to them, "You will get better as you go along, as you practice, as you learn and as you develop."

This is true for us, too. God is running the video camera along with the dads huddled over on the sides. But He is there encouraging our attempts, our flat voices and fumbling feet. And like a good Father, He too reminds us, "As you develop..."

I think our Father has "Daddy eyes." He sees the wobbles of our early attempts but He sees them in the whole picture of our developing dance. He isn't cringing with a playbill over His eyes. He's seeing each stumble and ungraceful trip as part of the artist's training. His "Daddy eyes" see the beauty of the whole play and our part in it.

I don't know what Heaven will be like, but if there are dancers, I have a sneaking suspicion that I'll end up being one of them. At the very least, I'll be dancing for a short while...

Dancing and Grooving
On This Earth for a Short While
Work Sheet

Theme: Our Christian Walk

Day One: Read full essay.

Day Two: What does this song say to you?

_____

_____

_____

_____

What in your life has made you interpret it this way?

_____

_____

_____

Day Three: What does the aerial view of *your* life dance look like?

_____

_____

_____

Are you happy with your life dance?

_____

_____

_____

Review Jesus' life dance in scripture, and see some examples of how He lived His.

Day Four: What have been the failures in your life dance?

_____

_____

_____

Are there any current failures you would like to change?

_____

_____

_____

What will you change?

_____

_____

_____

_____

How did Jesus confront difficulties in His life dance?

_____

_____

_____

_____

Day Five: What areas in your life would you like to develop?

_____

_____

_____

_____

How do they line up with scripture?

_____

_____

_____

_____

Find scriptures that support the changes you want to make.
What was the strongest character asset of Jesus' life dance (other than
    His divinity)?

_____

_____

_____

Day Six: Define "Daddy eyes" in your walk with God.

_____

_____

_____

How does He see your life dance?

_____

_____

_____

_____

_____

Does your life dance/Christian walk have any teeth in it?

_____

_____

_____

_____

_____

Does it speak to people who watch you?

_____

_____

_____

_____

_____

Day Seven: What would God tell you needs to be developed in your life dance?

_____

_____

_____

_____

Write a prayer for yourself about developing your life dance.

_____

_____

_____

_____

Make an index card listing the things you want to change in your life dance and place it where you will see it daily.

Ask friends to pray for your Christian development in these areas.

(Note: Use extra sheets of paper, if required.)

Saturday Night Fever

I don't know what you think of when you see *Saturday Night Fever* or hear its music, but the incredible dancing by John Travolta is *not* the first thing I remember. It's that awful white polyester leisure suit, silk shirt unbuttoned to the navel and the gold necklace. It's the finger pointing up and down as he struts. I wonder what we were thinking when we thought that look was cool? What were we thinking when we danced and sweated all night in polyester? That smell is worse than the after effects of puppy potty training. But it proves a point, doesn't it? It proves that we think whatever we are doing at the time is cool, right, hip, and prudent. We don't think we will come to regret any of those things. But how many of us have been the laughing stock amongst our children when they find pictures of us from the 70's...the guys sporting that leisure suit look and girls with the Farrah Fawcett hairdo's or the Cyndi Lauper 80's punk look? I know I will *never* live down my prom picture with Michael in his navy blue crushed velvet tux with a red, white, and blue paisley shirt underneath it! AHHHH! My stringy straight hair was no billboard for Teen Magazine.

According to me though, gosh, Michael looked good that night and I looked fabulous. We disco danced on those elevated, lit disco floors. It was cool, our clothes were cool, and the dancing was cool. File this under **never!** What were we thinking? In 2005, I'm not thinking much about the 70's was very cool. What will I be thinking in 2021? Will I think my opinions in 2005 were cool? Will I squirm each time I see a picture of myself at forty-three in some outfit that describes this era and think, "*What was I thinking?*" Yep, I probably will. This has given me pause for thought these days. What I am doing now...will it come to haunt me twenty years from now? What I think I know now, how will I think about it in twenty years? It is a humbling thought.

All of us get caught up in the moment and feel that whatever we are "passionate" about is the truth. It could be politics, a philosophy, a career, and even our denominational affiliation. This very well might be why the Psalms and Proverbs warn against living your life by mere passion. Wisdom is never attributed to choices by sheer emotion or by a consensus of your peers. We are reminded to line our passions up with the Word and then follow God's blueprint for healthy living.

I think this is obvious for my children who are now twenty-two and nineteen. I think it is **really** obvious when I hear Rap music or see Hip-Hop clothes. I know in my heart my kids will one day say about their generation "What were we thinking when we would absolutely die for those jeans that the crotch hung below our knees?" I smile, feeling vindicated about the crushed blue velvet tux.

Saturday Night Fever
Work Sheet

Theme: Our Christian Walk
Day One: Read full essay.
Day Two: What did you believe in, in the 70's?

_____

_____

_____

_____

_____

How much of that do you still believe in passionately?

_____

_____

_____

_____

Why?

_____

_____

_____

_____

Day Three: What did you believe in, in the 80's?

_____

_____

_____

How much of that do you still believe in passionately?

_____

_____

_____

_____

Why?

_____

_____

_____

Day Four: What did you believe in, in the 90's?

_____

_____

_____

How is that different from the themes of the 70's and 80's?

_____

_____

_____

How much of it was biblically based?

_____

_____

_____

_____

Day Five: What are four strong beliefs you have today? (They do not
  have to be religiously oriented.)

Ten years from now, which ones will stand as part of your true belief
  system?

What would Christ say about the four strong beliefs? Find it in scripture.

Day Six: Interview your best friend. What four strong beliefs do they
  hold?

Is there a theme that is relevant to this era? Are you simply getting
  caught up in the belief du jour?

What four strong beliefs does the Bible contend makes for a strong Christian walk?

_____

_____

_____

_____

_____

_____

_____

Support your answer with scripture.

_____

_____

_____

_____

_____

_____

_____

Day Seven: Pray and ask the Holy Spirit to reveal to you any defects in your Christian walk.

Write down what He tells you on an index card and post it somewhere that you can consistently pray about it.

Spend the next 20 minutes giving serious thought to the issues that you "thought" were so important in the 70's, 80's, 90's. How can you avoid being pulled in by the current fad of thought?

_____

_____

_____

_____

_____

_____

(Note: Use extra sheets of paper, if required.)

"Does It Hurt to Become Real?" Jesus the Velveteen Rabbit

The old skin horse answers, "When you are real, you don't mind that it hurts." I'm sure many of my counseling clients thought it was weird that I asked them to sit cross-legged on the floor as I read them the story of the *Velveteen Rabbit*. I'm also sure they wondered why they were paying me fifty bucks for the experience. I have used this book for 10 years in therapy and it hasn't failed me yet. It's a great metaphor for our lives and our fears.

The rabbit wanted to be real but he was afraid to be anything other than what he had been. The old skin horse was real and lived a life the newer toys wanted but were afraid to become. The old skin horse was played with the most because he was more real. He encouraged the rabbit by telling him "you don't mind if it hurts" when the handling gets a little rough. He is saying, the pay off to be real is worth it. I think this book is really for us adults who read it to our kids. Kids don't need the message. Kids are always real. It's us adults that learn to be "unreal," as we grow older.

Jesus was the most real person that ever lived. He dared to be the *Velveteen Rabbit*. Did it hurt? I guess so…He was crucified for being so real that the Pharisees didn't know what to make of Him. I had spent some of my life like the new toys, wondering what it would be like to be "real." I, like them, wondered if it would hurt to become "real." It did. But it was far worse being "unreal." The disciples finally lost their lives also when they became "real"—*radically real*. But they had come to know the cost of not being real, and it was easier to pay the cost of "realness" than it was to remain unused.

In the story, the rabbit sat on the shelf and watched the skin horse live life, be loved, used and played with. Some of us still live life today like that. Being "real"—*radically real,* will mean different things to each of us. Only the Holy Spirit can show us where we aren't "real." I spent a lot of years trying to be a "cookie cutter Christian." I can tell you that I am not one. I can't dress like them, act like them or role model those "mandatory" features that made me "fit" or "not fit" into some church systems. My being "real" in those types of systems mandated that I become "unreal." so I sat on the shelf and watched real Christian life go by me. I was unused. Risking being "real" for me meant being who I am in Christ, which may be different, from whom you are in Christ. My personality is different from yours; there are strengths in my personality that can be used. I had hidden away a lot of my realness; a lot of the strengths God gave me because it hurt being real. Initially it meant rejection, but eventually it meant finding a place in God's Kingdom where my gifts would be used. It meant being who I was and allowing God to place me where He wanted me, rather than me trying to fit in where I wasn't used and consequently, where I wasn't real.

"What is *real?*" the rabbit asks. The skin horse replies "Real isn't how you are made. It's a thing that happens to you." He goes on to say, "It doesn't happen all at once. You become." The skin horse reveals even more, "Once you are *real,* you can't become unreal again. It lasts for always." The rabbit longed to become *real*...he wished that he could become it with these uncomfortable things happening to him.

Being *radically real* costs us something. It has to. It cost Jesus something too. Its pay off is truth and authenticity. It is the availability to be used in ways that sometimes the world and even other Christians judge. It's a risk to be outside the "cookie cutter" norm. Jesus was not a "cookie cutter Jew." I couldn't live my Christian or counseling life in a suit. I couldn't operate in systems of rigid structure, which crushed individuality, whether in a church, a place of employment or in my personal life. I couldn't operate to my potential in places were my gender was more important than my love of God or where my career calling was highly suspect because it could not be documented in scripture in ways that they could understand. I couldn't continue to serve on boards that gave lip service to helping others but did nothing, or boards who thought I was "too risky" for helping the "un-helpables."

I've always lived close to the edge; it seems that's where God put me. I am my most real when I am by the edge, helping others who are over the edge. There have been a lot of judgments about that too but Jesus dared to live close to the edge. He was a ledge-walker so I felt I was in good company. Your own "un-realness" has to be shown to you by the Holy Spirit…the places He is calling you to be *radically real* to the Pharisees in your own life. Don't worry; Pharisees never know what to make of "real." Like the rabbit, we have to ask, "Will it hurt?" and like the skin horse, we will learn "When you are real, you don't mind that it hurts."

"Does It Hurt to Become Real?"
Work Sheet

Theme: Our Christian Walk
Day One: Read full essay.
Day Two: What is your fear about being "real"—*radically real?*

_____

_____

_____

_____

List a painful instance in which you risked being *real.*

_____

_____

_____

_____

What happened?

_____

_____

_____

Has that changed how you are real today?

_____

_____

_____

Day Three: Find three instances in scripture where Jesus was radically real.

_____

_____

_____

_____

What was the lesson taught to those who viewed His realness?

_____

_____

_____

_____

In these lessons, what could you learn to help you be *radically real?*

_____

_____

_____

Day Four: How is realness different from obnoxiousness?

_____

_____

_____

Give one example and show one ending as real and one ending as obnoxious.

_____

_____

_____

How does Christianity make you feel "unreal" sometimes?

_____

_____

_____

Day Five: How authentic do you think you are in front of other Christians?

_____

_____

_____

_____

What kind of Christians make you uncomfortable?

_____

_____

_____

_____

What kind of Christians make you feel "less than"?

_____

_____

_____

_____

Write a prayer for yourself asking the Lord to strengthen this part of
your walk.

_____

_____

_____

_____

_____

_____

_____

Day Six: How authentic is your walk in private?

_____

_____

_____

What is your current stumbling block?

_____

_____

_____

_____

What will you do about it?

_____

_____

_____

Do you live close to the edge?

_____
_____
_____
_____

How so?

_____
_____
_____
_____
_____

Why?

_____
_____
_____
_____

Day Seven: Write a one-paragraph biography on a current day Christian that you believe is radically real with a strong walk. Include what motivates you about them.

Post their name in your car to remind you of their walk.

_____
_____
_____
_____
_____
_____
_____
_____
_____
_____
_____
_____
_____

(Note: Use extra sheets of paper, if required.)

Deliverance—The Movie
and Otherwise

When I hear a banjo, I automatically think of the music from the movie *Deliverance*. I've heard all the *Deliverance* analogies, living in the mountains of western North Carolina. People wonder if I fear *Deliverance*-kind-of-people from here. Mostly I just fear *Deliverance*-kind-of-people not from here. What does that actually mean, *Deliverance*-kind-of-people? It conjures up images of inbreeding that produced men with square heads, tall foreheads and two of the brothers whose names are "Daryl."

The deliverance many of us don't think about when we hear the banjo is the kind of deliverance that might just change our lives. We all need deliverance of the heart from one thing or another. I need deliverance from prejudices that crop up when I least expect them and have stopped looking for them. I need deliverance from wrong attitudes and even less-than angelic motivations. Deliverance from impatience would benefit the entire work place. Deliverance from my double-edged tongue, *well*, that would delight my family.

My proclivity is to know what other people need to be delivered from. I can name the faults of all my best friends and close family members. I know how to pray for their deliverance, after all, if God listened to me they would be set free and a lot happier. But this in itself is what I need to be delivered from. If setting me deep in the back woods amongst moon shiners would change my heart I'd beat feet to the filming site of Deliverance, the movie; but I know the real deliverance is between God and me. When I name the thing to Him and leave it there, then I know that at the very least, deliverance has started in my heart.

I've got a lot to worry about just looking at myself. I don't have time to worry about square headed men coming over the mountain toward me. Even if they did, they might just be the banjo players I've been waiting on to teach me how to strum. What do I care if their names are "Larry, Daryl, and Daryl?"

Deliverance—The Movie and Otherwise
Work Sheet

Theme: Our Christian Walk
Day One: Read full essay.
Day Two: What does deliverance mean to you?

_____
_____
_____
_____

In your concept of deliverance, do you participate with God in it, OR does God only do it?

_____
_____
_____
_____

Find scripture to back up your belief.
Day Three: What in your life do you need deliverance from?

_____
_____
_____
_____

How is it affecting your Christian walk?

_____
_____
_____
_____

What would your kids/family say you need to be delivered from?

_____

_____

_____

Day Four: What is the one thing in your personality you just hate ?

_____

_____

_____

Do you think there is any opportunity to change it?

_____

_____

_____

Can you find a Bible character that had the same character flaw?

_____

_____

_____

What happened to them?

_____

_____

_____

Day Five: Write a prayer of deliverance for yourself.
Pray it for the rest of the week.

_____

_____

_____

_____

_____

Day Six: How did Jesus lead people into deliverance?

_____

_____

_____

_____

Use the Bible to find scriptural examples and write them here.
How can they be applied to you today?

_____

_____

_____

_____

_____

Day Seven: On this final day, how is your concept of deliverance different than when you began the study?

_____

_____

_____

_____

_____

_____

Are you more or less hopeful and why?

_____

_____

_____

_____

_____

Write a prayer to God about your request for deliverance. Possibly: Write an answer from God to you regarding your prayer requesting deliverance.

_____

_____

_____

_____

_____

_____

(Note: Use extra sheets of paper, if required.)

Character Development

Character determines destiny. This is why Christ has called us to His character and not our own. My own character has landed me in places I should not have been—places that wore me down or harmed me in some way. I do not need to build up my own character so that it simply lands me in more places I should not be, thus directing me toward a destiny I would not want. I need to become smaller inside myself so that Christ's character is given more place. I need less of me, and more of Him, as St. John discusses when he says, "I must decrease and He must increase." So the issue of destiny becomes extremely important…that is, if we want to land somewhere healthy.

Character development after one has accepted Christ is a paramount process. We cannot simply slide our toe over the line of salvation and hang out with our own gross inadequacies. Even the 12 Step traditions call us into a "fearless moral inventory" which requires that our character change. For it to change we must accept openly how it truly is at this moment. We have to accept that however it is it can be better as we grow into the likeness of Christ. We are not done and we will not be done until we are on the other side of this life. All of life is growing and changing. The good news is that Christ, as our role model, will develop our character into something that is mind-blowingly not us! And that is a *good* thing.

Unfortunately, the 60's, 70's and 80's taught us to see ourselves in ways that are myopic. And basically myopia isn't reality. We were spoon-fed so many "me-isms" that we wouldn't know ourselves if we stumbled upon our own psyches. The ironic part is that these eras were characterized by self-exploration or "finding our self experiences"; and the more time we spent digging around inside ourselves, the more lost we became. The maze that led us deeper and deeper into the navel-gazing of our own psyches and sin just convinced us of how groovy we really were. And for most of us, that wasn't true! "Finding ourselves," meant attaching to some levels of malignant narcissism that we never recovered from. Because Christ's way is always the opposite of the world, He tells us that in order to "find ourselves, we must lose ourselves." We spent years digging around inside to simply come up empty handed because the Truth we were seeking was not in us, but in Him.

The one thing I can honestly say after 30 years with Christ is that I am different. My character is, **thank God,** different. I am amusingly amazed to watch my life continue to change by just watching Christ as my example and allowing Him to implement that in my spirit. It's a cool process if you can sit back and enjoy the ride.

Stop steering. It's Holy Spirit driven.

The Unpleasant Realities of Sowing

"Sow a thought, and you reap an act;
Sow an act, and you reap a habit;
Sow a habit and you reap a character;
Sow a character and you reap a destiny."
(Chinese Proverb)

H uh uh…yuck, no way! Yes, way! What's truer than this? It's a lot of reality for this early in the morning, isn't it? Yeah, it is for me, too.

May I make a suggestion? Run get your Bible and write it on the inside cover. Now put it in your spouse's Bible too. God knows they could use it, right? Write it for the fridge door, a neighbor might come by and see it and could use it. Now put it inside your kid's backpack. What kid doesn't need to know this? Tape it to the dashboard of your car for when you are tempted to not wave with all five fingers. Put it on your desk at work when you are mumbling about that extra project that got assigned to you. And while you are at it, put it on your boss's desk so they know you are thinking about this daily. Send a little card to your pastor and put it inside. We know he knows this, but he might put it in next Sunday's bulletin where all those lazy-butts who don't volunteer to teach Sunday School will see it.

Xerox a bunch of them for insertion in your next Christmas card. It's better than those pictures of your dog with a Santa hat on. Embroider it on a pillow. We know that will last 'til eternity (or the next garage sale). Put in on your husband's golf bag to ward off character-destroying golf lies and curses on the golf course. Hang it in your local pub. It

might just send a few of them home to their families.... Have your lo-cal college make it their school motto for one year. It might be the end to some major college partying problems. E-mail your whole address book with it and ask that they pass it on—it's better than most of the crummy jokes you are getting E-mailed to you. Put it in every birthday and anniversary card you mail this year. Turn the saying into some kind of yard art so the neighbors learn this. Have an Urban Mural Project and paint it on the side of buildings in downtown; after all, this is a message for the masses. Assign it as a writing lesson to someone. Let it be a journal entry in your journal. Teach it in Sunday School class. There is a little old lady in there dying to learn it. Teach it in the teen youth group and change the future of America. Teach/preach it from the pulpit, and watch those who doze off perk right up. Talk about it at therapy. Your therapist definitely needs to hear this one. Paint a pic-ture that expresses it. Make it into a bumper sticker so the guy behind you learns it. Paint it as graffiti on your old clunker car.
Just do it.

The Unpleasant Realities of Sowing
Work Sheet

Theme: Character Development
Day One: Read full essay.
Day Two: From ages 0-14, what kinds of things did you sow?

_____

_____

_____

_____

_____

What kinds of things did you reap?

_____

_____

_____

_____

Is there anything from that time period that you are reaping today?

_____

_____

_____

_____

Look up scriptures on Reaping and Sowing in order to understand
how this principle works.

Day Three: From ages 14-21, what kinds of things did you sow?

_____

_____

_____

_____

What kinds of things did you reap?

_____

_____

_____

_____

Is there anything from that time period that you are reaping today?

_____

_____

_____

_____

What did you learn about how the principle works?

_____

_____

_____

_____

Day Four: From ages 21-30, what kinds of things did you sow?

_____

_____

_____

_____

What kinds of things did you reap?

_____
_____
_____
_____

Is there anything from that time period that you are reaping today?

_____
_____
_____

How do you feel about what you are reaping?

_____
_____
_____
_____

How can you make the principle work in your favor?

_____
_____
_____
_____

Day Five: From age 30 to the present, what kinds of things did you sow?

_____
_____
_____
_____

What kinds of things are you reaping?

_____
_____
_____
_____

How do you feel about what you are reaping?

_____
_____
_____

What do you want to change?

_____

_____

_____

_____

Day Six: Write a prayer about what has been sown in your life to this
point.

Ask God to help you sow the things that are healthy and God-honoring. Ask God to remove those things in your life that are unhealthy
and not God-honoring.

List all the things you sowed that were unhealthy:

_____

_____

_____

_____

_____

Day Seven: List all the things you have sown that are healthy:

_____

_____

_____

_____

_____

_____

List all the things you are committed to sowing in a healthy way for
the remainder of this year:

_____

_____

_____

_____

_____

_____

_____

(Note: Use extra sheets of paper, if required.)

Letting It Be

L ight patchouli incense and remember The Beatles with me…
hum along with me as I paraphrase them in their song "Let It
Be." "When the night is dark, a light still shines, shine even tomorrow, so just let it be." This was about as religious as many of us got
in the 60's and 70's. Hey, they did mention Mother Mary later in the
lyrics! And in the song "Rocky Raccoon," the infamous four even tell
us Rocky picked up Gideon's Bible and that Gideon was gonna work
with Rocky on his revival. Now, **yeah!** Ah, The Beatles—the only religion some would ever hear…not exactly the Ten Commandments or
the Nicene Creed, but there might be some speaking words of truth
and wisdom here for us.

Wisdom…letting it be…could it really be this easy? Three little
words "Let it be" turns this control freak's belly into more knots than
a sailor's rope. At forty-something, I am still trying to "Let it be" on
good insightful days. On bad clueless days, I am still trying to get the
world to line up with my own agenda and then feeling frustrated when
it doesn't happen. I'm sure it's "them" that are clueless, and I the en-
lightened one, with enough answers to solve the conflicts of the United
Nations. Although, solving world hunger is small compared to letting
it be on the mundane things of life like—"Mom, you look fat in that…"
or "Why **didn't** you get groceries on your way home?" Letting it be
on a professional level isn't any easier; especially when a colleague in-
sults my intelligence (and training) by saying, "We should ask someone who really knows…"

Countless times a day; little searing knife blades penetrate my body
(and ego) like acupuncture needles. A good insightful reframe for this
would be to say to myself, "Lots of opportunities present themselves
for learning to let it be." Could an empowered, quick witted, sarcasm

slinging, boundary-wielding therapist, **ever** be able to forfeit an opportunity to prove a point or elevate her own Woody Allen humor? Could she suck it up, let it slide, take it with a grain of salt, live and let live, or otherwise, *let it be?*

The Garden of Eden, the Christian Crusades, the Holocaust, the religious wars of Ireland, even the Clinton sex-capades; would any of them have existed if someone learned to *"let it be"?* With centuries of historical proof, it seems that human nature has a really hard time with letting it be. It appears I am not only normal, but in terrible company as well!

Christ's path was always a path of peace—letting it be. Willingly walking to the cross and getting nailed to it is the abject portrayal of letting it be. The Holy Spirit *lets it be* with us too, as we lollygag around in places we shouldn't be, until "the light shines on us." And as the song goes, "When the night is cloudy, there is still a light that shines on me" —He waits around, illuminating, letting it be. Of course some of us wander 40 years in the desert until we figure it out. *"Let it be"*—the need to be right, the striving for perfection, expecting others to not screw up, holding a grudge, being self righteous, being rigid, but most of all, white-knuckling life.

Four stoned rock musicians sitting cross-legged on the floor contemplating the meaning of the turbulent and violent times had a point. They knew we should "give peace a chance" but before we could ever do that, we'd have to learn to "Let It Be."

Letting It Be
Work Sheet

Theme: Character Development
Day One: Read full essay.
Day Two: How do you not *let it be?*

_____

_____

_____

_____

How would your friends say you do not *let it be?*"

_____

_____

_____

_____

What is Christ's example to us?

_____

_____

_____

_____

Day Three: Why do you not *let it be?*

_____

_____

_____

Why would your parents say you do not *let it be?*

_____

_____

_____

How did Christ let it be?

_____

_____

_____

_____

Day Four: What has your culture taught you about not controlling every aspect of your life?

_____

_____

_____

_____

Has it supported that belief or not?

_____

_____

_____

_____

How is culture like or not like scripture on this issue?

_____

_____

_____

_____

Day Five: Is your path a path of peace?
Was it always?

_____

_____

_____

_____

When wasn't it?

_____

_____

_____

_____

Why?

_____

_____

_____

What does a path of peace look like for you?

_____

_____

_____

_____

_____

Day Six: List five things you can do that you don't currently do to *let it be:*

_____

_____

_____

_____

_____

List three judgmental attitudes you have:

_____

_____

_____

_____

Write a prayer about your attitudes or any areas of non-peace in your life.

_____

_____

_____

_____

Day Seven: Find three separate Bible stories that show someone walking a path of peace, of *letting it be.*
What did you see that was different from you?

_____

_____

_____

_____

What can you implement?

_____

_____

_____

_____

Wherever You Go, There You Are

Over the years, many people came to counseling who wanted to leave a relationship, marriage, job, church, home, community or country. They thought that by leaving, things would "just some how get better." When you explore that a little deeper, you find they didn't have a clue or a plan how that would happen—they just hoped it would. We called that "magical thinking"—somehow they thought their problems would turn from a pumpkin into Cinderella's carriage, and just take them away from it all. We called that one the "geographic solution." If I get out of this, go there /leave here and go do that, it will all be ok.

It sounds like a good theory. It must, millions of people thought it to be a solution for their miseries. The real problem is, however, that you are your own problem. I used this quote a lot in counseling because it reveals the Adamic race. Not our racial lineage from Adam, but the race away from ourselves. When Adam and Eve sinned they began the restlessness that we have lived with ever since. They blamed others, even God, and Adam's heirs utilized the "geographic location" to try to solve their problems. Since sin, the Bible shows us story after story where people have tried to leave a relationship, marriage, job, church, home, community or country; but they are really running away from sin of self. And how do you ever really do that? Wherever you go, there you are…sin and self.

Pop psychology would tell you that you have to "make peace with who you are" but the Bible tells us we will never find peace in the lap of sin. We were made to feel yucky in the face of our sinful self. Christ is the only one who can stop the Adamic race; the fleeing from our very own selves. It is His redemption from sin and His peace that calms our battle with sin and self. It is His power that lets us have mastery over our own battles.

We could spend a lot of time running from relationship to relationship, from job to job—it always being someone else's problem that sets us running. But as my friend, Toni, eloquently put it to her teenaged daughter "You take yourself to the party."

Where Ever You Go, There You Are
Work Sheet

Theme: Character Development
Day One: Read full essay.
Day Two: What are you, currently, wanting to leave?

_____

_____

_____

_____

Why?

_____

_____

_____

What is your part in this/your responsibility to this issue?

_____

_____

_____

Day Three: Research five scriptures on commitment.
What did you learn?

_____

_____

_____

_____

_____

Has that changed how you see this situation?

_____

_____

_____

_____

_____

Day Four: List everything you have ever left:

_____

_____

_____

_____

_____

Research five scriptures on abandonment.
What did you learn?

_____

_____

_____

_____

Day Five: What are you running from?

_____

_____

_____

_____

What would your pastor say you are running from?

_____

_____

_____

What would your friend say you are running from?

_____

_____

_____

_____

What would God say you are running from?

_____

_____

_____

_____

_____

Day Six: Write a prayer asking God to help you stop running.

_____

_____

_____

_____

_____

Write a commitment statement to one thing you will stop running from:

_____

_____

_____

_____

_____

Become accountable to someone for this statement.

Day Seven: How has culture *not* supported the issue of commitment?

_____

_____

_____

_____

_____

What does culture teach about abandonment or your own level of un-comfortable-ness?

_____

_____

_____

_____

_____

What did Christ do about what He wanted to run away from?

_____

_____

_____

From what did Christ want to flee?

_____

_____

_____

How would life be different today if He had fled?

_____

_____

_____

_____

_____

_____

_____

_____

_____

_____

_____

_____

_____

_____

_____

_____

_____

_____

(Note: Use extra sheets of paper, if required.)

forever Younger

At fifty-something he's still sporting the spiked hair. Give it a rest, Rod. That's what I say. But hey, rival Mick Jaggar is still trying to wear a size 29 waist black leather pants, so what the heck. Age is real and these guys haven't embraced it yet. Us 60's, 70's, 80's rockers have gotta face that rockin' is now confined to porch swings. Forever young is something we told ourselves when we drove motorcycles too fast, did embarrassing kinds of things at parties and skipped school to contemplate our navels under the big blue sky. Forever young really isn't a concept for today, for me anyway. Of course, just a few days ago I wasn't thinking along those lines…

During a family vacation and a weak moment, I decided to ride the country's highest, longest and fastest wooden roller coaster. It was violent. It shook my head so hard that I received a slight concussion and had to leave immediately and go to the hotel room where we packed my head in ice. "Forever young?" I guess not. "Shake, Rattle and Roll" would have more likely been my theme song that day, not "Forever Young." Not even *a little young*! This was a big reality buster for me—my days of roller coasters, straddling Harley's and any other fast thing, were over.

The Proverbs talk a lot about youth. Most of it doesn't sound like they are promoting the vigor's of youth-but more like condemning the hair-brained, knee-jerk reactions that come with minimal amounts of age; rightfully so, since these are the things that tend to get us into trouble. Wisdom and the aged are promoted, which is why I like the book more and more each year. I wouldn't want to be *forever young*. In this age when people are chasing the Fountain of Youth, there is some comfort in knowing that I am getting older, and hopefully wiser.

My younger years produced a lot of fast-paced mistakes so slowing down allows me to think more. The Proverbs remind me, that despite Britney Spears' young face and Ally McBeal's anorexic look, it's ok to grow older. And according to the Book of Proverbs some benefits will also tag along listed as promises, which include a long life, the spouse of your youth, kids who return to honor you, and yes—wisdom. Sorry Rod, no spiked hair was mentioned. And Mick, no black leather pants either. Give it a rest, guys.

forever Younger
Work Sheet

Theme: Character Development
Day One: Read full essay.
Day Two: How do you feel about your current age?

_____

_____

_____

_____

Is this how you thought you would feel?

_____

_____

_____

_____

Why?

_____

_____

_____

_____

Day Three: How did you feel about your age in your teens?

_____

_____

_____

_____

How is that different?

_____
_____
_____
_____

How do you hope to feel about the next 10 years?

_____
_____
_____
_____

Day Four: What does scripture say about age and wisdom?

_____
_____
_____
_____

How wise do you think you are?

_____
_____
_____

How wise would your pastor say you are?

_____
_____
_____
_____

Write a prayer asking for wisdom.

_____
_____
_____
_____

Day Five: What are some of the promises that scripture makes about age and longevity?

_____

_____

_____

_____

_____

How does that affect your self-concept at this age?

_____

_____

_____

_____

How did Jesus view age?

_____

_____

_____

_____

Day Six: How old do you feel inside?

_____

_____

_____

_____

Do your chronological age and the age you feel inside ever clash? Why?

_____

_____

_____

_____

What does culture teach about age and youth?

_____

_____

_____

_____

Day Seven: How wise were you in your youth?

_____

_____

_____

_____

_____

What do you regret?

_____

_____

_____

_____

_____

Write a prayer asking for forgiveness for what you did in your youth.

_____

_____

_____

_____

_____

Write a statement of anticipation for the next ten years.

_____

_____

_____

_____

_____

Write what you hope to be like then.

_____

_____

_____

_____

_____

_____

_____

(Note: Use extra sheets of paper, if required.)

Stand-ing!

S ly and The Family Stone knew a lot more about "standing" with others than we did. Boomers are notoriously characterized by our ability to "keep our options open." It's our own created cliché to avoid saying that we fear commitment and trust. We are, after all, the generation that vowed to not "trust anyone over the age of 30." If we have vowed anything it is to "go with the flow" "if it feels good, do it" and to "live and let live." We began the national trend of 50% divorce rates, personal debt that exceeds yearly income, moving every five years and the lowest volunteer rate in fifty years. We have not been the role models of monastic maturity. And we have changed how America lives life and what we are willing to commit to.

Perhaps this is why I was all the more shocked to find a statement by a community that was committed to the notion of "stability." Written by an "intentional Christian community" who live a shared life, they made a "vow of stability" to one another, to their community and to their church. This is actually not a new vow. This is a vow taken from the Benedictine Tradition in monasteries that has existed and been vowed now for centuries. It only seems odd today because stability is often equated with the concept of "boredom."

It caught my eye too as a therapist. It thrilled me to think of the implications of "vowing stability." It would have made counseling a lot quicker and my career a lot shorter if people could really grasp it! I envisioned psych hospitals closing, civil courts disbanded, and child support offices boarded up. Communities flourished and met each other's needs. Churches grew and lacked nothing. How would life change if we vowed stability to our partners, our children, our friends, our neighborhoods and our churches? How would life change if we vowed stability spiritually, financially, psychologically and sexually?

How would we grow if we knew we would be with these people the rest of our lives, period? That is the "vow of stability"—to live with and care for these people until death. Not until it doesn't feel good any more, not until the first disagreement, not until the better opportunity happens along, not until greener pastures, not until finances wane, not until churches crumble. But we vow to stay WHILE we are disillusioned, while we are angry, while we are hurt, while we are confused and while we don't want to be there.

We vow to stay and let ourselves be rubbed raw into growth. Only community can rub us right into a leap of spiritual growth.

Stability is a sign of maturity. It is a sign of commitment and covenant. It is a sign that is the opposite of a boomer worldview. But the Benedictine's don't worry much about personality conflicts and differences within their communities. They know they have a lifetime to work it all out. They know despite it all, they are all there for the long haul. Their confidence is not in themselves as mediators of their own personality-challenged community, but in the Holy Spirit who is the sanctifier of all. And in the process that is at the very heart of the "vow of stability": the willingness to allow the rubbing to force you into sanctified spaces you might never otherwise grow into. If there are no loopholes, such as ones that were created by civil courts for divorce, what might happen to us? What might we have to do in order to work it out? Might we forgive, or give, or hold our tongue, or give wise council, or hug someone, or listen, or cry with or cry alone, might we dig deep inside ourselves to see what it is about US that makes this situation difficult? Might we beg forgiveness, own our faults, pray for and with another, and plead for our own sanctification? Might we look the other way, lend a hand and shoulder and heart and dig our feet in and refuse to be moved from our stable life?

Stability: the ability to care for and nurture one another, forever. Amen.

Stand-ing!
Work Sheet

Theme: Character Development
Day One: Read full essay.
Day Two: List five things you are committed to:

_____
_____ 🖊 _____
_____
_____
_____

From this list, list five ways you have violated your own commitment
to these things:

_____
_____
_____
_____
_____

Day Three: What were you committed to in your 20's?

_____
_____
_____
_____

In your 30's?

_____
_____
_____

In your 40's? (if applicable)

_____
_____
_____
_____

How are these different from each era?

_____

_____

_____

_____

_____

Day Four: What are you stable in today?

_____

_____

_____

_____

What are you not stable in?

_____

_____

_____

_____

How has culture supported/not supported the issue of stability?

_____

_____

_____

What did Jesus' stability look like?

_____

_____

_____

Day Five: How would your life change if you vowed stability in your: Spirituality?

_____

_____

_____

Relationships?

_____

_____

_____

_____

Finances?

_____

_____

_____

_____

Mental Health?

_____

_____

_____

_____

Sexually?

_____

_____

_____

_____

Day Six: What would change if you dared to stay in something that would rub you into growth?

_____

_____

_____

_____

_____

What would that be?

_____

_____

_____

_____

Why are you running from it?

_____

_____

_____

_____

_____

How does Christ model this issue of stability and commitment to us?

_____

_____

_____

_____

_____

Day Seven: Write a prayer asking God to show you areas that you are not stable or committed in.

_____

_____

_____

_____

_____

_____

_____

Share these with an accountability partner.

List how you will change what God showed you:

_____

_____

_____

_____

_____

_____

(Note: Use extra sheets of paper, if required.)

"I Am Sam, Sam I Am"
(From *Green Eggs and Ham*, Dr. Seuss)

I have a really cool friend named Sam. Sam is an associate youth minister at the church we attended together. He is the kind of guy people flock to and he has great people skills. The whole family is one big "out reach" of sorts. Somewhere along the line this family learned the message about caring and reaching out. Their whole life seems to be geared in this fashion. They are always analyzing what new program they can use to help others. I know that Satan would like nothing better than for them to not reach out to other people and his plan is to side-track any who are wanting to minister to the needs of others.

When I first met Sam, I recognized a lot of great talent in him. He had been home schooled and then was stricken with a critical illness. He hadn't gotten around to a GED following that. I began to encourage him to think about doing something with his life. Just because he had some deficits from the illness didn't mean he couldn't have a career. At first Sam showed interest in either counseling or youth pastorate, which fit his great people skills. He began the process of jumping through the hoops of the local community college to get his GED, then his college testing, which would eventually require him taking some basic classes before he would have to decide what career he wanted. Before too long Satan was all involved in Sam's career plans. Sam got interested in a "get rich quick" kind of real estate deal. It had all the bells and whistles that a 22-year-old would find attractive. Dip it in a little hopeful thinking and a promise to help other people through this endeavor, and Sam was fairly convinced this is what God would have him do.

A year later, Sam is still waiting and the real estate deal hasn't gone through "yet" although he still talks about it as a "possibility." The Angel of Light who held a beacon that shined on a "possibility" stole a whole year from him. I talked to him about how Satan makes things appear so promising that it takes us off track from what the Lord wants us to do. College is less appealing than owning a million-dollar piece of property, granted. But sometimes God is not always calling us to the things that seem grand.

Satan knows which bells and whistles appeal to our own passions. He waves them in our face hoping that our more primitive nature will be drawn to it. Meanwhile, years roll off the calendar as we chase the rabbit, only to find precious time has been lost in our service to the Lord. Our prayer for our own selves needs to include the ability to follow the Lord's plan for us. The things that appear to be grand might just turn out to be a thief in the night.

"I Am Sam, Sam I Am"
Work Sheet

Theme: Character Development
Day One: Read full essay.
Day Two: List your top five passions:

_____

_____

_____

_____

_____

_____

How do you satisfy those passions?

_____

_____

_____

_____

_____

_____

How much time is given to those passions?

_____

_____

_____

How did Christ use His passion?

_____

_____

_____

_____

Day Three: What are your strengths?

_____

_____

_____

How do you use those daily?

_____

_____

_____

How do you use those for God?

_____

_____

_____

If you do not, why don't you?

_____

_____

_____

How did Christ use His strengths?

_____

_____

_____

_____

_____

Day Four: What is God calling you to?

_____

_____

_____

_____

How are you avoiding that?

_____

_____

_____

_____

Why are you avoiding that?

_____

_____

_____

_____

What are you doing to accomplish what God is calling you to?

_____

_____

_____

_____

Day Five: Describe how culture validates/invalidates passion.

_____

_____

_____

_____

_____

Describe how culture validates/invalidates calling.

_____

_____

_____

_____

_____

How is that affecting moving ahead in your calling?

_____

_____

_____

_____

_____

List a Bible story that shows passions leading someone wayward and
what the outcome was:

_____

_____

_____

_____

_____

Day Six: List a Bible story that shows a calling that was fulfilled and
what the outcome was:

_____

_____

_____

_____

_____

How did Christ fulfill His calling?

_____

_____

_____

_____

_____

Write a prayer asking God to help you recognize and fulfill whatever calling He has for your life.

_____

_____

_____

_____

_____

Become accountable to someone for answering the call in your life.
Day Seven: What in your character is holding you back from fulfilling your calling, or utilizing your strengths for God?

_____

_____

_____

_____

_____

List five things you can do to move ahead in this area:

_____

_____

_____

_____

_____

What does scripture say about fulfilling your destiny in God?

_____

_____

_____

_____

_____

(Note: Use extra sheets of paper, if required.)

Discipleship

It matters what we grow into. That is why the Lord made a big deal about it and why the issue of discipleship is important. You will be the disciple of someone or something. That is human nature—we follow. (Haven't all the fads since the 60's proven that point?) So being sure that you are following *whom* and *what* you want to follow is important. The question is do you know *whom* or *what* you are following? Are you sure?

Jesus' command to us was to "go into the world and make disciples." So, therefore He has taken a great interest in that occurring in us and through us. It is perhaps the most critical aspect of our spiritual formation following our salvation. Our discipleship will probably determine several things: how well we continue to grow in depth in the Lord, whether we will consider a calling in some sort of Christian service, how we will or will not live out the gospel in our personal life, and how we develop critical thinking skills.

Discipleship is really an on-going growth pattern, that is, we continue to grow into the likeness of Christ. This will require reviewing our character defects, allowing God to remove them, living authentically and openly, being accountable for the quality of our lives, and practicing the various spiritual disciplines. You can see why it takes the rest of our life to work on these things!

These are critical issues for boomers, X-ers and Y-ers who have been raised on a pop culture devoid of serving others. Our pop culture turned us self-ward; and so scripture challenges us with Truth when it tells us to turn our focus on God and others. It feels odd to see this as Truth when life so far had been about feeding our senses through the mall, movies, MTV, cable, the internet…and now we are told to look elsewhere for meaning and purpose.

But discipling doesn't have to be all stuffy and confining. God uses our real lives in order to teach us about His life. We've just got to develop the eyes that see where God really hangs out—and that's in our lives. Just look! He's there in the frustration and humor of raising our kids, at the three-ring circus we call our workplace, in all the dynamics of our personal relationships, and even in the work He is trying to do in our heart…He's there.

I hope these essays shed some humor on the whole issue of being Christ-like, after all, it feels like a pretty gargantuan task. The Lord shares our giggles as well as our ogles when it comes to this.

The Road Less Traveled or The Gate is Narrow
(By M. Scott Peck)
(Matthew 7:14)

Any counselor in their right mind loved M. Scott Peck. He rattled our apathy with insight. Over the years, he forced us to look at things such as; the source of choices, whether evil really exists, issues of integrity and the importance of community building. He enlarged our capacity to see God in our midst, in our offices, in our relationships...and also His absence in our midst, offices and relationships. He's an author that can make you squirm, so he's my kind of guy.

He broke onto the writing scene with *The Road Less Traveled*, a title that caught us as it reflected the famous poem by Robert Frost. It's been my motto most of my life. Friends have called it "eccentric" "stupid" or "fun" depending on their own risk level. But really, it's just a family trait. Most of my family has lived rather unconventionally as musicians, starving artists or gypsy wanna-be's. My life as a counselor and writer would probably have been even a little stuffy for the likes of my dad, a jazz musician.

Nothing has been more unconventional than being a Christian. Jesus is a radical guy. His road is less traveled because of its radicalness. He referred to His road as a "narrow gate" with "few" that pass through it. We don't have to worry about the "Y" in the road and which way to choose but rather whether our ego and heart will fit through The Narrow Gate.

As opposed to New Age Theory, which suggests that "many paths lead to God," Jesus informs us that not only is it only **one** path that leads there but on top of it, it's mighty narrow and few go there. It truly is *The Road Less Traveled*. And with good reason...it includes sacrifice, discipline, prayer, giving, study, self-denial and other forms of less culturally fun frivolity. It's not a theology or theory you would invent if you wanted to make one up, which is exactly what gives it its authenticity. If you want a road, street, highway or byway you'll have to pick something other than Christianity. He only offers a gate.

The Road Less Traveled/The Gate Is Narrow
Work Sheet

Theme: Discipleship

Day One: Read full essay.

Day Two: What was unconventional about your life before you be-came a Christian?

_____

_____

_____

_____

_____

What is unconventional about your life now that you are a Christian?

_____

_____

_____

_____

What does the world call unconventional?

_____

_____

_____

_____

How does your life fit/not fit with the world's account of it?

_____

_____

_____

_____

Day Three: What is the most radical thing about Christ?

_____

_____

_____

_____

What is the most radical thing about your own Christianity?

_____

_____

_____

_____

How can you use your radical-ness for good?

_____

_____

_____

_____

What Bible character do you relate to regarding radical-ness?

_____

_____

_____

_____

_____

Day Four: Read Matt 7:14
How has the gate been narrow for you?

_____

_____

_____

_____

How has the gate to destruction been wide for you?

_____

_____

_____

_____

What can you learn about gates?

_____

_____

_____

_____

_____

Day Five: Will your ego fit through the gate?

_____

_____

_____

_____

_____

What do you need to lay down in order for your ego to fit through the narrow gate?

_____

_____

_____

_____

_____

Share this with your accountability partner.
Will your heart fit through the gate?

_____

_____

_____

_____

_____

What do you need to work on in your heart so it fits through the narrow gate?

_____

_____

_____

_____

_____

Share this with your accountability partner.

Day Six: Find the scripture that says that there is only one path to God and write it here:

_____

_____

_____

_____

What does that path require of us?

_____

_____

_____

_____

How are you fulfilling/not fulfilling that?

_____

_____

_____

Day Seven: Examine your own commitment to discipline.
What is your commitment to discipline?

_____

_____

_____

Examine your own commitment to prayer.
What is your commitment to prayer?

_____

_____

What culturally fun frivolity do you feel God is calling you to examine?

_____

_____

(Note: Use extra sheets of paper, if required.)

Peace, Peace
When There Is No Peace
(Jeremiah 6:14)

No peace here. Not anymore. It's 7:15 A.M. on a weekend and on my front porch a 130-pound Akita wrestles a 70-pound Akita puppy with the flips of the Federated Wrestling Commission. On my back porch, two cats imitate "Taz" by whirling, chasing and knocking over plants. In the yard I see a remnant of a tennis shoe that was last night's entertainment. Foam from the shoe is scattered on the deck. On my back deck, I see a little dead something and bend over to make out what it "use to be"; a baby bat.

The perfect morning I envisioned is **not**. After separating dog fights and cat fights, my morning will consist of yard and porch clean up. What do you do with a dead bat? I flash to my early 20's…I remember peaceful mornings then…peace in general.

I also flash to the phrase "Cultivate Peace" from some bumper sticker I saw recently. I think, "File that under *never*—they don't live in *this* house." I stare at a pair of hormonally large dogs and a pair of manic cats. How can peace be here, now?

The disciples had the same challenge—to find peace in the moment. Not peace in the chaotic world around them; but peace in themselves as they lived in the chaotic world. We know that until the New Jerusalem is established this is pretty much what we've got to work with… and it gets worse as the world progresses. So, the world and its chaos are not going to change. We can only change ourselves. The only peace we can bring to the table is the peace inside ourselves.

What if we adopted that as a spiritual discipline for six months? What if we took responsibility for our own level of peace daily; monitored it, tended it, cultivated more of it, grew it larger and deeper, and gave it immediate attention when it waned? What if, everyday, our peace was our objective?

Jesus is called The Prince of Peace. He learned something about the necessity of a peaceful heart. He had to learn to maintain it through all the heated and asinine interactions with the Pharisees, the teachings to simpleminded disciples and in relationships with needy followers. He had to find it in the crucifixion when He asked the Father to forgive those who were killing Him. Even in the middle of His death, the peacefulness had a voice.

I must remember this when two big muddy dogs jump on me in my work clothes, when my hormones are doing back flips and when I am whinny and discontent. But for the next week, let's make peace our objective; give it the attention we give to Seinfeld reruns. Who knows?

Peace, Peace When There Is No Peace
Work Sheet

Theme: Discipleship
Day One: Read full essay.
Day Two: Define your concept of peace:

_____
_____
_____
_____
_____

Define the world's concept of peace:

_____
_____
_____
_____
_____

Define Christ's concept of peace:

_____
_____
_____
_____

Research and list five scriptures on peace:

_____
_____
_____
_____

Day Three: Define your concept of chaos:

_____
_____
_____
_____

Define the world's concept of chaos:

_____
_____
_____
_____

Define Christ's concept of chaos:

_____
_____
_____
_____

Research and list five scriptures on chaos/unrest/non-peacefulness:

_____
_____
_____
_____

Day Four: What did you learn from your research?

_____
_____
_____
_____

How do you cultivate peace in your own life?

_____

_____

_____

_____

How consistent are you with it?

_____

_____

_____

_____

Will you make peace a spiritual discipline for yourself for the next six
  months?

_____

_____

_____

_____

How will you do that?

_____

_____

_____

_____

Day Five: How will you be responsible for your peace on a daily basis?

_____

_____

_____

_____

_____

How will you monitor it?

_____

_____

_____

_____

_____

How will you cultivate more peace in your life?

_____

_____

_____

_____

_____

What area of your life do you really need to work on in order for peace
to be daily habit?

_____

_____

_____

_____

Day Six: Discuss peace with your accountability partner and what you
plan to do about it.
What did Christ do to cultivate peace in His life?

_____

_____

_____

_____

_____

How can you use that in your search for peace?

_____

_____

_____

_____

How does your lack of peace, effect others?

_____

_____

_____

_____

Ask three people how it affects them, and write it here:

_____
_____
_____
_____
_____
_____
_____
_____

Day Seven: What are you committed to doing about the issue of peace?

_____
_____
_____
_____

How much silence do you have in your day (absolute silence)?

_____
_____
_____
_____

How can you add some?

_____
_____
_____
_____

Will you add some?

_____
_____
_____

Biscuits Don't Count
(A familiar saying in these here mountains)

"Miss Lessie, what'd ya have fer breakfast dis mawnin'?" the nurse asks.

"Nuddin" she says while looking pitiful.

"Nuddin. Really? Yun's need to et sum'in or ya will waste way ta nuddin."

"Nuddin. I jest had me some bizkits."

"Well, that ain't nuddin."

Back at my office a couple of cohorts say, "We're gonna run to the Huddle House and pick up some breakfast. Want any? I didn't have anything today yet, just a couple of bizkits." The other says, "Heck, they don't count."

I ask a patient, "Beulah, what's making your blood sugar run so high, do you know?"

"Naw, I don't know."

"Well, you know you can't eat a lot of sugar or carbohydrates, especially early in the morning. What did you eat?"

"I haven't had breakfast yet. I'm still waitin' to eat."

"Your aide hasn't gotten you breakfast yet? It's 11 A.M."

"Well, I just had a couple of bizkits, but they's nuddin."

I didn't realize that biscuits have zero calories or I would have started eating them a long time ago. It's the latest joke in our house these days when Ken wants to fix a big Sunday breakfast. He yells, "Do you girls want bizkits? You know they don't count!" Lauren, always looking for a free calorie says, "Sure!"

Aren't we sometimes just like this when it comes to sin? We like to think, "That one doesn't count." We've created our own reality when we assign zero calorie accountability to our sin. A little white lie here, a small indiscretion there, a rationalization like, "No one tells the truth to Uncle Sam anyway." Pretty soon most of our untruthful day has added up to a big zero when it comes to a sin tally, at least in our minds.

Jesus looks at it a little different than a zero, and His call on it is a little hard to take sometimes. He said if we even THINK it in our heart, we have done it. Our hand doesn't even have to be in the cookie jar to be nabbed…our heart just has to wish it were. In the long run it's a good way to keep up with yourself because if you are monitoring your heart, your hand isn't likely to run astray. The end of the day sin tally isn't likely to be 683, but on your arithmetic scale it isn't likely to be zero either.

Biscuits might not count in these here mountains, but some things do!

Biscuits Don't Count
Work Sheet

Theme: Discipleship
Day One: Read full essay.
Day Two: What habit or sin are you denying in your life?

_____

_____

_____

What would your partner say you are denying?

_____

_____

_____

What would your kids say you are denying?

_____

_____

_____

What would God say you are denying?

_____

_____

_____

_____

Write the "ouchiest" ones here:

_____

_____

_____

_____

Day Three: Rate your own sin.
On a scale of 1-10 (10 being high) rate the sin you are denying:

_____

_____

_____

_____

Rate the sin your partner would say you are denying:

_____

_____

_____

_____

Rate the sin your kids say you are denying:

_____

_____

_____

_____

Rate the sin God says you are denying:

_____

_____

_____

What did you learn?

_____

_____

_____

Day Four: Research scripture and find someone who denied their sin even when they were confronted with it.

What scripture did you find?

_____
_____
_____

Describe the story:

_____
_____
_____
_____
_____
_____

What was the outcome?

_____
_____
_____
_____

Day Five: How could this outcome end up being your outcome?

_____
_____
_____
_____

How could this outcome *not* end up being your outcome?

_____
_____
_____
_____

Name five proactive things you can do about this:

_____
_____
_____
_____
_____

Day Six: Meet with your accountability partner and discuss these denials.

Discuss options (12 steps, a group, counseling, etc.).

What options did you discuss?

_____

_____

_____

_____

_____

_____

Which one(s) are you going to do?

_____

_____

_____

_____

_____

Day Seven: How did Christ deal with people's denial?

_____

_____

_____

_____

Research scripture and list an example here:

_____

_____

_____

_____

_____

Write a prayer asking God to help you end your denial.

_____

_____

_____

_____

(Note: Use extra sheets of paper, if required.)

Living Your Life by the Little Soaps Theory

I was watching a documentary on middle-aged women who were doing a very dangerous rafting trip in Colorado as some sort of rite-of-
passage thing to help them face their fear of aging. I thought they
were a lot braver than me, given the violence of that river against them.
It helped them face something just as big in themselves: illusion.

They interviewed the women at the beginning, middle, and the end
of the trip. Many discussed the challenges of the river as metaphors for
the challenges of menopause—both raging kinds of things that felt out
of control. They emerged feeling like they could at least live through
these things, if not conquer them. That seemed a fair enough appraisal
of both types of raging rivers.

One woman when asked why she chose *this* as her vacation said,
"I didn't want to go some place where there were little soaps. I wanted
something more to challenge my life with."

Little soaps! How many of us live our lives wanting a "little soap"
life? Little pink rose bud soaps in a hand painted porcelain soap dish
that sits next to your sink. We all know they never get used. We are
always waiting for a special occasion, or someone more significant than
us, or our family to use them. What is it that we think we want in a
"little soap" life; comfort, safety, the pretension of English properness?
My little soaps always looked crusted up with dark dust that clogged
up the carvings in the rose design. They weren't attractive any more.
Of course, we still didn't use them either.

This woman was saying she wanted to go somewhere that represent-
ed the opposite of "little soap" living. She wanted to smell fear, conquer
challenges, and go where women feared to tread. She wanted to face the

unknown, embrace ambiguity, and chase after Truth. I couldn't help but think she should have tried Christianity. Jesus wasn't a "little soap" guy. Christianity shouldn't be a life of "little soaps" either—comfort, safety and the pretension of properness. If our Christian journey resembles "little soaps" more than it does a rugged ride down the Colorado River, we need to toss those soaps. The Christian journey should be full of rites-of-passages that make us face, like these women, our own illusions. Ditch the soap; you'll never use them anyway.

Living Your Life by the Little Soaps Theory
Work Sheet

Theme: Discipleship
Day One: Read full essay.
Day Two: What rite-of-passage are you facing now in your life?

_____

_____

_____

_____

How have you been dealing with it/not dealing with it?

_____

_____

_____

_____

How would you like to deal with it?

_____

_____

_____

Day Three: In scripture, find someone else who is facing what you face. What did you find?

_____

_____

_____

_____

How did they deal with it?

_____

_____

_____

Can you apply it to your situation?

_____

_____

_____

Day Four: Describe your own desires for a life of comfort:

_____

_____

_____

How do you think this desire was developed in you?

_____

_____

_____

How do you see that line up/not line up with scripture?

_____

_____

_____

Day Five: Describe your own desires for a life of safety:

_____

_____

_____

How do you think this desire was developed in you?

_____

_____

_____

How do you see that line up/not line up with scripture?

_____

_____

_____

_____

Day Six: Describe your own desires for a life of pretension:

_____

_____

_____

_____

How do you think this desire was developed in you?

_____

_____

_____

_____

How do you see that line up/not line up with scripture?

_____

_____

_____

_____

Day Seven: Write a prayer asking God for an authentic life.

_____

_____

_____

_____

Ask him to show you the areas in your life that are false fronts.
Write them here:

_____

_____

_____

_____

Transfer them to a post-it note and put it on your mirror.
(Note: Use extra sheets of paper, if required.)

"If You Have a Skeleton in Your Closet..."

"...take it out and dance with it," Carolyn McKensie tells us! You might as well...it's better than the door flinging open one day and it falling out in the middle of your anniversary party, your kids finding it and being frightened by it, or your spouse pulling it down on their head while trying to get the bowling ball off the shelf. This much we know is true: skeletons have a way of showing up at the most inopportune times and they tend to have a big mouth, too.

Dancing with it is not suggesting that you flaunt it and act like its existence is a big nothing. It is merely suggesting that it be exposed and no longer hidden. Skeletons that are properly introduced to the family are no longer feared as inappropriate anniversary party attendees nor scary things that pop out at your kids and topple off of shelves. They are flapping on the clothes line in the open air. People wave at them and step over them, they prop them in the corner at the party, or lay their coats on them. They are part of the environment that is accepted. No shock-eroos here.

Jesus is the embodiment of full Truth. There is nothing that exists in Him that isn't truth. That's why He's so hard to take, and why the Pharisees where blown over by His mere presence. That much Truth glaring you in the face can cause you to squint. Jesus asks us to walk that journey of truthfulness because when we do, we are touching something of Him, sharing in His life, His death and representing all of who He is. Of course, it doesn't hurt either that truth keeps our closets cleaned out.

Next time the closet door cracks open and you see an eyeball peeking out, jerk that door open and grab that skeleton by the hand and say, "Will it be the tango or the fox trot?"

"If You Have a Skeleton in Your Closet..."
Work Sheet

Theme: Discipleship
Day One: Read full essay.
Day Two: What is currently in your closet?

_____

_____

_____

_____

_____

What three things do you fear most about what is in your closet?

_____

_____

_____

_____

Day Three: How have you handled closet secrets in the past?

_____

_____

_____

_____

How do you want to handle them today?

_____

_____

_____

_____

What do you need to do in order to handle them the way you want
 to?

_____

_____

_____

Day Four: Research five scriptures on truth.
What did you learn?

_____

_____

_____

_____

How did Christ confront untruth or deception?

_____

_____

_____

Day Five: Write a prayer asking God to help you handle your secrets
 better.

_____

_____

_____

_____

_____

Take one step toward handling your skeletons the way you really want
 to.
What is that step you are going to take today?

_____

_____

_____

_____

Day Six: Talk with your accountability partner about one of your secrets.

How did that turn out?

_____

_____

_____

_____

What scripture, that you researched earlier, can help you at this
time?

_____

_____

_____

_____

Day Seven: Do you remember a time in your life when you lived with
no skeletons in the closet?

_____

_____

_____

_____

When was that?

_____

_____

_____

_____

How did that feel then, compared to now?

_____

_____

_____

What is your commitment regarding this?

_____

_____

_____

_____

"I Am The Potter, You Are The Clay"
(God)

This year my mother, who is a potter and sculptor, "insisted" that I begin this insane so-called "art form" of pottery. She lugged 25 pounds of clay in on her hip, like she would a two-year-old toddler, and slung it on my table. She savagely ripped off a hunk throwing it onto a covered-board. She mashed, rolled, threw, and squished this blob until I thought my 25-year-old kitchen table would fall to the ground from gyration. Then began "THE" instructions: "You have to hit it like this, get all the air bubbles out, roll it out with a rolling pin, don't let it dry out, it can't be too wet, don't let it stick to the rolling pin, make sure you use enough clay, don't use too much clay or it will dry out, use the heal of your hand, get your fingers into it, let it do what it wants to, and get a feel for the clay's agenda." I've had a hard enough time dealing with my own subconscious agendas without having to worry about what clays wants to do with theirs!

As I worked late into the night at this clay thing, I was really thinking this wasn't nearly as much fun as the Play Doh Factory™ I had as a kid. You just inserted the shape you wanted, mashed the handle and viola—Kiddy Art squeezed out into pleasurable and distinct geometric shapes! It was a no-brainer. Not so with clay if you decided to try to attach the title "Potter" to yourself in this woman-against-clay battle.

With only a master's degree, I was clearly not smart enough to learn the mechanics of molding mud. Out came the gadgets associated with the agenda-carrying clay. The gadgets are used to help you force the clay into conforming to *your* agenda for it (after I had clearly been instructed to "go with" the clay's agenda). There are dangerous looking wires that can cut through 25 pounds of clay like butter, scalpels that surgeons would envy, special sponges and molds, soft brushes and hard ones, and glazes that cover the entire color spectrum. There are "rules" for firing it too—this heat or that, and "rules" for drying it. You have to know the differences in mud-made-into-an-art-form: high firing clay vs. low firing clay, clays used for porcelain, clay used for food dishes, clays that work in this kiln or that one. Then there are the processes—wheel thrown or hand built mud; not to mention all the disasters in glazing to learn, if you want to know why the piece you worked on longer than your thesis looks like kindergarten art. I clearly was not ever going to live long enough to learn how to make mere mud mind me.

After I had spent more time molding mud than it took me to write a 300 page book, I loaded it into my car for a drive to the next town to have it fired. There I learned that they don't fire pottery that arrives in tiny pieces and dust from breaking on the way to the kiln. Back and forth weekly I went—wet pottery to be fired, back home to glaze it, back to the kiln to be fired, pick it up and bring it home. My Day Timer had enough entries of when to pick up and drop off, that this "hobby" resembled a full time job.

My house was strewn with clay from end to end. Big tables were erected in the basement for drying, another on the porch for creating and glazing, the floor of the porch for glaze drying, the kitchen counter for acrylic drying. As I sat on the porch "creating" one day, cursing the clay and my aching hands and back, it occurred to me that being called clay by God was *no* compliment. I had battled mud all day, ignoring its "agenda," trying to make it curl here or flatten out there, stay moist and stop cracking, when I realized this wasn't a very satisfying adventure...and probably not for God either.

I thought of my life as "mere mud" in God's hand. He had tried to squish out the air bubbles (or hot air I should say) more than once to keep me from drying out, mold me into a beautiful vase vessel, while I, the clay, had my own agenda. I folded over when He wanted me to lie flat. I lay limp when He was curling me up, heavenward. Making something beautiful out of hardheaded clay isn't easy. God too, as a Masterful Potter, respected the clay's agenda. In His mind's eye, He had a stately vessel envisioned. The clay, of course, had another idea: lay limp, dry out, crack, and fold the wrong way.

One neat thing I did learn about clay, that God obviously knows, is that when you make something that doesn't turn out, you can reconstitute the clay. It can be re-submerged in water (you know, Living Water) where it becomes even more pliable than it was originally. This incredibly soft clay is less resistant, has less of its own agenda, is less dry and can be shaped easier than its former condition. Hmmmmm...

I guess that's what some of us mud monsters need—to be reconstituted, re-submerged in Living Water, to be made softer and more pliable in the Potter's hands. I've got a lot more respect for God's work as a Potter now that I've battled mud. I just wonder if God ever thought the Play Doh Factory™ would have been easier....

"I Am the Potter, You Are the Clay"
Work Sheet

Theme: Discipleship
Day One: Read full essay.
Day Two: Describe God's role as Potter in your life:

_____

_____

_____

_____

_____

_____

Describe incidents in which He acted as Potter:

_____

_____

_____

_____

_____

Day Three: Find the passage in scripture that refers to God being "the Potter" and read it.

Is there a metaphor for how this relates in your life?

_____

_____

_____

_____

Day Four: How did Jesus allow God to "shape" Him?

_____

_____

_____

How has God shaped you in the past?

_____

_____

_____

What do you think He is trying to shape in you currently?

_____

_____

_____

_____

Are you cooperating or resisting?

_____

_____

_____

_____

Day Five: Research your favorite Bible character and see if you can identify this metaphor at work in their life story.

How did God "shape" them?

_____

_____

_____

_____

What similarities do you see for yourself?

_____

_____

_____

_____

Day Six: Write a prayer asking to be made cooperative in this shaping process:

_____

_____

_____

_____

What areas are you pliable in?

_____

_____

_____

_____

What areas are you hard in?

_____

_____

_____

_____

Day Seven: Tell your accountability partner what areas you are hard
in.
Discuss ways of allowing God to mold you and shape you.
What do you hope the outcome is for your "shaping"?

_____

_____

_____

_____

What one thing do you want to see happen because of this?

_____

_____

_____

(Note: Use extra sheets of paper, if required.)

Garage Sale Begins
Saturday at 9 A.M.

W e're moving again. This statement brings fear and trembling to any friend or family member of ours that has helped us move in the past. They have horrible flashbacks to moving episodes at times when I owned nine couches. But each moving experience has turned into a kind of spiritual retreat. I go through my too cramped garage and begin a flurry of pitching. (I tell my husband I would make a great furniture bulimic.) Then I take stock of "why" I own this much stuff. I repent. Throwing food away with thoughts of children who are starving doesn't move me the way throwing away stuff clients have given me or some little memento of a victorious time in my life does. So I re-evaluate "what" can go this time. (I repent again.) I am ruthless! Out goes thank you cards, letters of successful therapy, client gifts of knick-knacks along with beds and bed frames, a grandfather clock, and two desks. Timber, my puppy, runs by and I ponder if he should go in the garage sale too. Then I move from thinking about "what" to "who's"—this is my stuff but what about Ken's? Let me get into his. Out goes a ban saw, a shop vac...the adrenaline is pumping now. What else can I drag to the curb to get rid of?

Then the Holy Spirit whispers, "What about pride? Can you drag that to the curb and dump it? Or all that impatience with Lauren you had this week? You don't need that any more. I think you've worn out those opinions you spout at work—put them together in a big bag. How about 50 cents for your grumbling? What do you say we pitch this restlessness—you've used it for years and look, it's all worn out on the edges? Oh—over there, I found a big pile of envy. It looks in pretty good shape. Do you want it?"

With trepidation I tell Him, "Well—ok—you can get rid of it all. Shall I help you?" I ask.

"No, I can do it myself." He answers.

Later I tell my husband, "I think this is going to be our best garage sale yet!"

Garage Sale Begins Saturday at 9 a.m.
Work Sheet

Theme: Discipleship

Day One: Read full essay.

Day Two: Pray and ask the Holy Spirit to reveal to you what needs to be gotten rid of in your life.

Sit quietly and listen.

Write down what He said:

_____

_____

_____

_____

_____

_____

Day Three: Take item number one from the list you made on day Two. Describe why this is a problem in your life:

_____

_____

_____

_____

_____

Who else would say it is a problem in your life?

_____

_____

_____

_____

_____

Day Four: Pray and ask the Holy Spirit to remove that defect that you
identified yesterday.

Take item number two from the list above. Describe why this is a problem in your life:

_____

_____

_____

_____

_____

Who else would say it is a problem in your life?

_____

_____

_____

_____

Day Five: Pray and ask the Holy Spirit to remove that defect that you
identified yesterday.

Speak with your accountability partner about these specific things the
Holy Spirit revealed to you.

Discuss with your accountability partner what you can proactively do
about this.

What did you decide?

_____

_____

_____

_____

_____

_____

_____

_____

_____

_____

Day Six: Take item number three from the list above. Describe why this is a problem in your life:

_____

_____

_____

_____

_____

_____

Who else would say it is a problem in your life?

_____

_____

_____

_____

_____

Research scripture and find Bible characters that had these same problems in their lives.
Who are they?

_____

_____

_____

_____

_____

_____

How did they handle it?

_____

_____

_____

_____

_____

_____

_____

Day Seven: Pray and ask the Holy Spirit to remove the defect that
   you identified yesterday.
What did you learn from the Bible characters?

_____

_____

_____

_____

_____

_____

_____

_____

_____

Is there something they did that you can apply to your own situation?

_____

_____

_____

_____

_____

_____

_____

What will you do?

_____

_____

_____

_____

_____

_____

_____

_____

_____

Illumination of Scriptures and Theology Formation

Theology Formation seems so forbearing. The issue is just way too big. It seems stuffy, rigid and frankly, B-O-R-I-N-G! It's as big as the universe and how will one ever conquer it? Illuminating Scriptures seems like an oxymoron! The word "Scripture" in and of itself seems to mean "un-understandable" so how do you illuminate the illusive meaning? Deep down in our worldview of scripture and church things, we believe only nerds really want to know this stuff anyway. That's what I believed and was shocked to find myself getting an undergraduate degree in Theology. I kept saying out loud like I was in some drug-induced state, "What am I doing here? This isn't me." I was sure I was a victim of the old movie *Invasion of the Body Snatchers* and my real self had been stolen away by some scripture thief that was trying to hypnotize me with theology. It was very scary at the time but I was able to convince myself that theology was no more than the ancient art of storytelling. What I was learning were historical stories about our past. Whew! It relieved a lot of stress to look at it that way.

So we begin this segment of our study looking at issues surrounding scripture and theology. The reason this is important, is that we are only as healthy as our theology. We most certainly have seen the truth of this over the years as we have witnessed the atrocities committed in cults—Heaven's Gate and David Koresh, Charlie Manson, Jim Jones, Osama Bin Ladin, and others. This is the epitome of theology gone bad.

The roots of our belief system are important to understand because they influence the development of our theology. This is why the first segment in Our Christian Walk was looking at some of the belief systems we brought with us into Christianity. Without sorting through these, they have the propensity of tainting our theology in subtle ways.

Our theology was formed in our early and teen years. Did you realize that? Even the years we were not in church were years of theology formation, because if we do not actively seek to form our theology based on healthy teaching, culture will define it for us. And so the 60's, 70's, and 80's all formed a theology in the space in our hearts and minds that had been God-shaped. I remember nights at parties in high school where we would smoke pot and read the Book of Revelation out loud. It was the closest thing we could find to true horror to get thrilled about. Even in my stupor, it was a theology class that would take **years** of real theology classes to over ride what I learned in those times.

We bring to our churches all that Joplin and Hendrix taught us. We bring what Vietnam preached; and what LSD taught us about the "other world." If you weren't that "wild" then maybe you bring what the peace marches taught or the idealism of capitalism; but we all have the propensity of bringing a subversive theology with us. When we try to superimpose our theology over the top of it, it doesn't line up. We end up frustrated and confused. A faulty theology must be dismantled and a healthy one rebuilt. We must lay aside fear and assumptions about the stuffiness of this theology building. We can take an easier ride toward it than what we have been telling ourselves.

"Do not adjust your set! This is the Outer Limits!"

Bye-Bye Ms. American Pie

Are you brave enough to admit to yourself and Don McLean you haven't a clue what "Bye-Bye Miss American Pie" is about? I am. I remember in high school telling my boyfriend, as I loudly belted out the song to the car radio, "What the heck is this song about?" He didn't know either. My husband swears he understands this song. I doubt it—he says it's about James Dean's death or maybe about Marilyn Monroe. Yeah, whatever—after all, art is highly subjective.

I hear people say the same thing about the Bible, "it's hard to read and understand" and "it's subjective." Sounds like Dick Clark's Band Stand™—"It's hard to dance to and I don't like the beat." Well, as opposed to the reasons behind Don McLean's song, the Bible DOES have a reason for its quirkiness.

If you don't like mysteries, you won't like this answer. The Bible is cloaked in a spiritual mystery; not the kind from Alfred Hitchcock movies where fog rises from the bog…but the kind where until your spiritual pilot light is lit by the Holy Spirit, the Bible remains garbled. Without 3-D glasses, why see a 3-D movie? You miss the cool effects if you aren't seeing it thru the 3-D eyes.

It's the same thing with the Bible; until you have asked Christ to illuminate the scriptures for you through a relationship with Him, the Bible remains a mystery that is "hard to dance to and has a difficult beat." Christ is "the lamp unto our feet and a light unto our path." He's the 3-D glasses. It's His book. He authored it through a conglomeration of others, and He knows best how it should be read and interpreted. He says we need the 3-D glasses to really "get it." It's His artwork and after all, art is highly subjective. But if you want it to be easy to dance to and have a good beat, ask the Guy who wrote it.

Bye-Bye Ms. American Pie
Work Sheet

Theme: Illumination of Scripture and Theology Formation
Day One: Read full essay.
Day Two: Is the Bible hard for you to understand?

_____

_____

What makes it difficult?

_____

_____

_____

_____

What is the hardest part to understand?

_____

_____

_____

Day Three: What does the scripture "All scripture is God breathed"
  mean to you?

_____

_____

_____

_____

How much time per week do you spend on helping yourself understand
  scripture in deeper ways?

_____

_____

_____

How can you help yourself go deeper?

_____

_____

_____

_____

Day Four: What preconceived ideas about scripture do you bring into the relationship with God?

_____

_____

What has your past taught you about scripture?

_____

_____

Is this impeding your ability to see scripture differently?

_____

_____

Day Five: What is your concept of the 3-D glasses?

_____

_____

_____

Do you believe God can illuminate scripture to you?

_____

_____

_____

Have you had this experience?

_____

_____

_____

Do you want this experience?

_____

_____

Pray a prayer asking God to help you understand scripture through the power of the Holy Spirit.

Day Six: Using a concordance, look up five scriptures that reveal God's viewpoint about His own work (the scriptures).
How does this apply to what you have been looking at all week?

_____

_____

_____

_____

What did you learn?

_____

_____

_____

Day Seven: Using a concordance, look up five scriptures that reveal Jesus' viewpoint about scripture.
How does His view differ from yours?

_____

_____

_____

_____

Do you feel any differently about scripture after looking at it all week?
What has changed?

_____

_____

_____

What do you want to change?

_____

_____

_____

What will you do to bring that change about?

_____

_____

_____

(Note: Use extra sheets of paper, if required.)

Oh God, Will Ya Get Me A Mercedes Benz?

Although Janis Joplin didn't write it, she did sing it in her throaty kind of way. Janis must have heard a little "Prosperity Theology" preached in her day. It got her going naming all the stuff she wanted to pry out of God. She thought a little song and a little prayer would turn her world into a party!

"Prosperity Theology" or "Comfort Theology" has been looked at from all angles since boomers started lining the seats of pews. We brought with us the strange mandate for clergy to tell us what we wanted to hear. As a hardheaded generation it was hard to get us into the pew and keep us and perhaps this was the advent of the Prosperity Theology.

Janis must have got us thinking about it in the 60's when she asked God for a Mercedes, a color TV, and a little drinking money. She, like many, equated what God gave her with how much He loved her.

"Name it and claim it." "Blab it and grab it." "Want it and flaunt it." "See it and believe it".

It's all gone under many little cliché names over the years and we've all seen the truth of it revealed in the excesses of some Tele-evangelists. But sometimes we don't see it in our own church or our own home. We live in the most prosperous and abundant nation on earth. It is no wonder we can't differentiate a need from a want. I attended a church that was pedaling Prosperity Theology. One of the associate ministers told me, "I want to be a **good** steward of God's money so therefore I am going to buy a Mercedes because they hardly ever break down and they easily will run until almost 200,000 miles." (Sounds like Janis, doesn't it?) My response about the car was, "Well, a VW Beetle meets that criteria too, but I don't see you racing to be a **good** steward in that direction."

For myself, I do not believe in the current presentation of Prosperity Theology. The universality of the scriptures is proven by the ability of scripture to be true among every nation, tribe and tongue. That is why many are converted on all continents; because the basis of the Bible rings true, everywhere. If Prosperity Theology were **really** part of the truth of the gospels, it would be true in Bangladesh. As they pray, naming and claiming, where are their houses, jobs and cars? Where is the abundance poured out in their country? Is it a lack of faith, lack of knowledge, lack of prayerfulness? Theologians agree that when any one part of the New Testament scriptures is used exclusively for a people group then it is probably not true. If prosperity is not for the third world nations, what is God saying?

I loved Janis Joplin in the 60's and 70's. It's just that my theology has grown a little since then. I don't use it to measure whether I think God loves me or not, like Janis did. God's Word is true—He does meet my needs. Last month I wondered how I would make my mortgage payment, due to a slow month with our cabin rentals. But low and behold a weird insurance rebate check came and viola! He has come through again! I've never lacked food, shelter, love, friends and a church family. That is the True Prosperity and Comfort that He promised.

Oh God Will Ya Get Me A Mercedes Benz
Work Sheet

Theme: Illumination of Scripture and Theology Formation
Day One: Read full essay.
Day Two: What was your parent's relationship with money like?

_____

_____

_____

_____

_____

_____

What were you raised to believe about money?

_____

_____

_____

How is it the same/different today?

_____

_____

_____

Day Three: How is your relationship with money today?

_____

_____

_____

How is your debt situation?

_____

_____

_____

Is this reflected in your relationship with money?

_____

_____

_____

Day Four: What does the Bible say about money? Review five scriptures.

_____

_____

_____

What does the Lord say about guaranteeing your prosperity?

_____

_____

_____

Write a prayer asking the Lord to teach you about these areas.

_____

_____

_____

_____

Day Five: How important is overall "comfort" to you?

_____

_____

_____

_____

What does "Deny yourself, pick up your cross and follow Me" mean to you?

_____

_____

_____

_____

Where is your comfort line in giving it all away to serve Christ with no material objects?

_____

_____

_____

_____

Are you comfortable with where you are at with this?

_____

_____

_____

_____

Day Six: What conclusions can we draw from Christ's examples of how He lived His life?

_____

_____

_____

_____

_____

What was His relationship with money like?

_____

_____

_____

What was His relationship to the idea of "comfort" like?

_____

_____

_____

Day Seven: What message do you think you have received from culture about prosperity, money, and comfort?

_____

_____

_____

Do you want your children to learn the same messages from culture that you have learned?

_____

_____

_____

Why or why not?

_____

_____

_____

What can you do to reform your (and your children's) outlook on these areas?

_____

_____

_____

(Note: Use extra sheets of paper, if required.)

It Is Costly Wisdom, Brought By Experience Part I
(Roger Aschram)

I remember thinking that I wish it didn't hurt so much to be wise. That was pretty good insight for a teen. I was an adolescent and one of my favorite TV shows was, *Kung Fu*. My friends thought it was stupid that I would rush home to watch it. I liked it because the main character had grasped some deeper truths in his childhood about life that kept being re-enforced week after week by all the knuckle brains he kept encountering. Each week I began watching with a kind of sadness, sensing it would cost him something to walk out or realize his wisdom. If he doubted anything he had learned previously, each episode illuminated what it had cost him to gain the knowledge he now has. Isn't that true for all of us?

It costs us something every time we learn or grow. We only realize we have learned something by the experience that brought the insight. Wisdom is not static. We don't acquire wisdom outside of experience. It is the experience coupled with insight that brings about wisdom. We've all had experiences that taught us nothing because there was no insight. We've also had experiences that taught us when the insight finally emerged. The reality of wisdom is that we tend to learn the deepest truths about our self and God in experiences we have labeled "uncomfortable" or down right painful. These experiences are the ones most likely to be passed over as only an "aggravation" or "an attack of the enemy." We risk the loss of wisdom each time we release an experience without the insight.

A few years ago I was submerged in immense emotional pain. The only thing I was acutely aware of was the pain of the present moment and my circumstances. Various friends were helpless, except to remind me that I was learning something in the wilderness. At that moment, it didn't help because pain is egocentric. We only desire to be out of pain. A friend said to me, "Where is the gift in this?" It was the right timing, serving as an ice water submersion experience—startling! On the surface none of this felt like a gift: one daughter was in rehab, my husband and I were separated, my marriage on the verge of death, God distant and cold, and my other daughter angry and hurt.

I rolled that over and over in my mind and compared it to scriptures that reminded me that all things, even painful, worked together for this insight thing. The Old Testament reminded me to "seek wisdom" as more precious than gold or silver. I stood at the crossroads of opportunity, not just the opportunity of putting my family back together, but at the crossroads of wisdom and insight that would bypass whatever happened in my family. I could release this experience as "their problems and behaviors" or I could wrestle out the insight that illuminated my own character defects, how this experience spoke deeply about other issues in our lives, how it revealed where we needed to go as a family and what it said about what God was doing in our hearts.

It is Costly Wisdom Brought by Experience Part I
Work Sheet

Theme: Illumination of Scripture and Theology Formation
Day One: Read full essay.
Day Two: What wisdom in your life was brought by experience?

_____

_____

_____

What is your view on the benefits of wisdom?

_____

_____

_____

_____

Day Three: What did you learn from the experience?

_____

_____

_____

_____

_____

How have you used what you learned from the experience?

_____

_____

_____

_____

_____

Day Four: Look up five scriptures on wisdom.
What is the predominant theme amongst the scriptures about wisdom?

_____

_____

_____

_____

_____

How can you relate that to your life?

_____

_____

_____

_____

Day Five: Who is the wisest human you know?

_____

_____

_____

_____

Why do you think they are wise?

_____

_____

_____

_____

What have they taught you?

_____

_____

Day Six: What experiences have occurred in which you did not get wisdom?

_____

_____

_____

_____

Why not?

_____

_____

Did you seek to learn something at the time from the experience?

_____

_____

What have you since learned?

_____

_____

_____

Day Seven: Write a prayer asking for wisdom to be given to you.

_____

_____

_____

What do you believe your role is in the stewardship of your own wisdom?

_____

_____

_____

(Note: Use extra sheets of paper, if required.)

It Is Costly Wisdom, Brought
By Experience Part II
(Roger Aschram)

I had the opportunity to forego the insight and allow the experience to be only what it was—extremely painful. On the surface, it would have been easy to do. The behavior of others in the family lent to the obvious deterioration of our lives together. I could have thrown my hands up and said, "I have no control over what they choose or don't choose." While that was true, the deeper issue was "Am I going to learn from this, whatever the outcome?" Would I choose to walk away with wisdom brought by this emotional death experience or would I leave the wisdom behind veiled in blame, logic and excuses?

I don't remember making a conscious decision to embrace the wisdom of these experiences, but I must have opened myself up to considering the concept enough that it led me there. When I'm in pain, I usually go back and read Thomas Merton books. It was there that Merton reminded me about adversity being our primary teacher in life, never by choice. He spoke of our character being revealed in times of pain and that wisdom is achieved by knowing who we are in the pain as it illuminates our own weakness. The wisdom of the experience was unexpected. I "expected" to learn about Lindsay, Lauren and Ken and all that had collapsed leading us to this pain.

What I did learn as I looked at my own weakness was about me and profoundly, about God. The illumination of my own defects in fact, illuminated God's grace in ways I had never before experienced. Perhaps there is a two-sided wisdom we learn in experiences: one, about our own weakness, that is, to see our real defects; and the other is about God's grace and character in the midst of our own failings. The amazing part was that as I allowed insight about myself; I grew in insight about God. We each faced our real selves of profound weakness and saw God's love, for the preservation of this family. Each of us, in truth, never expected to come out of this as an intact family. As we each sought wisdom from this "year of Hell." the family reunited in stronger ways; in the arms of grace, God's and ours, for each other. We learned about the fragile ecosystem of a family's life that needs to be ever balanced to survive. Our own self-exploration of our roles in the break down of our family life taught us not only about ourselves, but also each other. And it will continue to teach us about God as we become more and more aware of what actually happened in that terrible year and in us because of it.

All four of us paid a great price of experience for what we learned that year. The gratefulness is the "wisdom that was brought by the experience." I don't want to go back to that year again—ever! But there is a great promise in the 12 Steps that says, "You will come to not regret anything you lived." And so it is that we lived, we survived and we learned; and like Kung Fu, we know what it cost us to know what we know...

It is Costly Wisdom Brought by Experience Part II
Work Sheet

Theme: Illumination of Scripture and Theology Formation
Day One: Read full essay.
Day Two: How do you make other people wrong so you don't have to look at your own hand in the problem?

Do you think this is forsaking the wisdom that could come in this
situation?

_____

_____

_____

How could you do it differently?

_____

_____

_____

Day Three: How aware do you stay of your own defects?

_____

_____

_____

_____

How has this hurt you?

_____

_____

_____

If you were more aware, what would happen?

_____

_____

_____

Day Four: List five character defects.

_____

_____

_____

Which ones are affecting your family the most?

_____

_____

_____

What will you do about it?

_____

_____

_____

Day Five: Which character defects are affecting your spiritual development?

_____

_____

_____

How did Jesus manifest His wisdom?

_____

_____

_____

Find three separate instances of Jesus' wisdom being walked out. What can you learn from it?

_____

_____

_____

How can you apply it in your life?

_____

_____

_____

Day Six: Find three separate instances of other Bible characters acting out of wisdom.
What occurred in their lives previously that gave them this wisdom?

_____

_____

_____

_____

List how is this the same as/different from your situation?

_____

_____

_____

Day Seven: Ask your best friend to tell you what they wish you had learned from a situation. Just listen. Do not debate it.
Compare it to what you have learned about yourself through this chapter(s).
(Note: Use extra sheets of paper, if required.)

Step One: Read the Instruction Booklet

My husband hates to read instructions. I often wonder if this is a genetically predisposed wiring in men that after they have broken the thing they are trying to put together, then they dig the instructions out of the garbage for a little help. He figures he's got a 50/50 chance that he won't need the help it offers. He's got a 50/50 chance that the thing he puts together for his family's use won't collapse and kill them if he's put it together wrong. He's got some slim chance (about the same margin of chance that he will win the lottery without buying a ticket) that he will never in the future ever need the instructions, so why keep them?

I think we think the same thing about the scriptures. The Bible is our Instruction Booklet for putting together this thing we call a "Life" but some of us don't ever get around to reading it for the help it offers. We figure, like Ken, that we've got a 50/50 chance that we won't need what it tells us we *do* need. We've got a 50/50 chance that if we put our life together according to our own guesses, that maybe it won't collapse and kill our family; and we might have the slimmest of chances (about the same margin of chance that we will win the lottery without buying a ticket) that we will ever need the instructions in the future, so why read them?

More than once I've seen my husband's fanny perched high in the air as he's digging in the garbage can praying the instructions are still in there. From my standpoint, I still think it's silly he doesn't read them beforehand and save all this back tracking, grunting, digging and praying. He hates to admit that maybe he needs a little peak, at least at the diagrams.

How many of us will feel safe about our kids playing on a gym set that was put together with one screw? "Ah heck, it'll probably hold…" Or swinging from a porch swing tacked up with pushpins? How many of us like the feeling in the pit of our stomach when the thing is put together, there is a pile of "extra parts" and the person who put it together thinks that they don't go into the object? Clue: Them's not extras!

Step One: Read and follow the instructions to ensure proper safety.

Step One: Read the Instruction Booklet
Work Sheet

Theme: Illumination of Scripture and Theology Formation

Day One: Read full essay.

Day Two: What do you believe about the necessity of understanding the Bible and its influence on the outcome of your life?

_____

_____

_____

_____

_____

Why do you believe this?

_____

_____

_____

_____

Make a reminder card that suggests that you make time to spend in the scriptures. Place it where you can see it all week.

Day Three: How much time do you think you should spend daily in growing your own spiritual development?

_____

_____

_____

_____

_____

How much time do you spend?

_____

_____

_____

What do you want to spend?

_____

_____

_____

Day Four: What does Jesus say about the importance of scripture?

_____

_____

_____

_____

_____

How did He use scripture in His life?

_____

_____

_____

How is it used with Satan?

_____

_____

_____

_____

Day Five: How would your pastor say you are doing in your spiritual development through the application of scripture?

_____

_____

_____

What did you formerly believe about scripture when you were in your 20's?

_____

_____

_____

What about in your 30's?

_____

_____

_____

How will it change in the next ten years?

_____

_____

_____

Day Six: Name five things from the Bible that are helpful in understanding the journey of life.

_____

_____

_____

Name three areas you wish the Bible helped more in.

_____

_____

_____

Name one person that is further along in spiritual development that could help you look more closely at those three areas.

_____

_____

_____

Day Seven: Call the person who is further along in spiritual development and make an appointment to discuss how they use scripture for their own growth.

Make a plan to increase your reading time to fit with where you feel you need to be spiritually.

(Note: Use extra sheets of paper, if required.)

Lord of the flies

It was 1974 and I was a junior in high school. We had just read *Utopia* and *Animal Farm*. It was fun reading and good discussion. It was the end of the year when *Lord of the Flies* was ordered as our final book. It was a freaky book for a teen whose bent was towards peace and the sociology of a gentle world.

After a few chapters, I was scared for Piggy, the emotionally and physically weakest of the bunch. I was even more scared to watch sort of normal kids in the book turn into psychopaths. I wondered if our teacher was making non-verbal comparisons after our rowdy behavior earlier in the year. Our project for this book was to produce a piece of artwork that would tell part of the story.

The problem was, I was getting too freaked out to finish the book, so I bribed a class member, Tom, whose affections were being directed my way, to do the project for me. He was a fabulous artist and a brave soul who thought the book was "cool." He drew a pencil collage of Piggy's face in various scenes of the book. All of the faces were ones of horror. The drawing was so detailed it was traumatic.

Although I skipped scary parts of the book, it was still discussed in detail in class. I got the gist of it, unfortunately. The book made me fearful that a chaotic world, without balance, could at any time, turn evil, and destroy the weaker ones. This was a lot of reality for a 16-year-old, and a pretty good theology at that. Most of the boys didn't think that would happen, ever. A quiet timid girl in the class spoke up and reminded us that "history repeats itself" and this had already occurred. She said to study this closer we should examine both the Bible, which shows this happens repeatedly when civilizations chose atheism, and to study the Holocaust when civilizations chose anarchy. The room was silent as death…Piggy's death. The class bell rung and summer officially began. She got an "A" in the class. I went back to church that summer.

Lord of the Flies
Work Sheet

Theme: Illumination of Scripture and Theology Formation
Day One: Read full essay.
Day Two: What, about the world, scares you?

_____

_____

_____

_____

_____

Do you view the world as "chaotic without balance?"

_____

_____

_____

_____

How have you seen the world change in the last twenty years?

_____

_____

_____

_____

Day Three: What do you fear most about the changes in the world?

_____

_____

_____

_____

What does Jesus say about how the world will change?

_____

_____

_____

_____

_____

What hope does He offer?

_____

_____

_____

_____

_____

Day Four: What has happened in cultures where atheism was dominant?

_____

_____

_____

_____

_____

What does scripture say about atheism and chaos?

_____

_____

_____

_____

Day Five: What examples can you give of cultures that lived in anarchy?

_____

_____

_____

_____

_____

Compare and contrast Christianity with anarchy.
Is there any anarchy in your life?

_____
_____
_____
_____
_____
_____

Day Six: Would your family say there is anarchy in your life?

_____
_____
_____
_____
_____
_____

What is the most noticeable factor about anarchy?

_____
_____
_____
_____
_____
_____

Is that noticeable in your relationships?

_____
_____
_____
_____
_____
_____
_____

Day Seven: Pray and ask Christ to show you any areas of your life
  which need changing.

Chaos can also be in our homes, not just in the world. Where is it in
  your life?

_____

_____

_____

_____

_____

_____

_____

_____

_____

_____

_____

_____

_____

_____

_____

How can you change that?

_____

_____

_____

_____

_____

_____

_____

_____

_____

_____

_____

The Body of Christ

There is nothing more mystical, magical, and mandatory than our functioning within The Body of Christ. At the time of our salvation, we inherit a whopping big family that spans thousands of years. We have lineage that winds all the way back to the first disciples and looms by light-years in the eternal future. It's a cool thought to think of all those who we are now related to by spirit; and as with any family, we've got to figure out how to get along, how to mind our manners, and support one another in this big family reunion. Instead of interacting like a Jerry Springer™ show, we've got to figure out our place in this family and honor that by doing our part. We've got to bring to our new family all of our strengths, that in turn strengthens our whole family. It isn't that we can't bring all of our hurts and "baggage" as it is to our family. In a healthy family, there is room for everyone to "come as they are." But we must also see not only what we can draw from the family in support, but what we can give to the family in strength.

This ability to bring strength to the family ties in to the chapter on Discipleship. How we grow in Christ has a lot to do with the character we bring to this new family. Also critical to our functioning within the Body of Christ, is for us to develop a realistic outlook of what The Body is. Many come to Christianity with an outlook that expects perfection and are "shocked" to find just ordinary folk amongst our ranks; and some gnarly kind of people at that! We expect the pews to be filled with Billy Grahams and Mother Teresas, but we never count on finding Woody Allen or Hawkeye there. Like the title of the book,

it is Moody Pews—those of us that cross cultures, eras and upbring-
ings to line the pews with attitudes that range from Woodstock to the
Peace Corp.

How we function in The Body of Christ is really more important
than who we are. We don't like to hear that, given our own evaluation
of our self-importance, but role and ranking in this Body is less important than our ability to function healthily; so we must learn how
to be a healthy family member in an organization that looks "fringe"
at best. We're going to be paired up with some strange folk and it's our
job to figure out how to grow in this environment and how to help our
brothers and sisters grow too. This will require all sorts of skills from
us. So we'd better get started in really looking at all of us who make
up this Body of Christ.

We Are the Army of God

The other morning our pastor preached that God chose us to be in His army. For some reason this was a very humorous concept. The only army that I could think of, or the only one He would invite me into, was M*A*S*H*. You remember those ragtag knuckle-brained participants: martini drinking-woman-chasing Hawkeye, adulterous and wimpy Major Frank Burns, the other-woman Hotlips, adolescent Radar, cross-dressing Klinger, solid-to-the-core Colonel Potter, and the rest of them? It didn't appear to me to be an impressive army, or a scary one, that could challenge the world and win.

The M*A*S*H* crew was seriously flawed individuals with funny personality quirks, but in the end, had a real devotion to their work. I guess that's been the Christian Army from early on. It seems that God keeps picking the same kinds of people over and over again for this job so He must have some purpose in His picking. He has consistently **not** picked the high and mighty ranking individuals who would woo the world. You might say God has picked the comical over the academically serious.

Our first prototype of the Army of God was the first disciples. **Ha!** Here is a snap shot of the first Army and the Armies who followed after them: Impetus Peter whose big mouth and knee jerk reactions caused constant clean up in the politics of Jesus, and he was not unlike Hawkeye who required constant supervision due to his mouth; weirdo John who was so strange that he was considered more delusional than holy and whose mode of dress in that day might not have been too far off from Klinger's dress in M*A*S*H*; Judas who was the internal Mafia man selling secrets and Jesus' life to guys like Guido, who resembled Frank Burns' constant betrayal of the holy tent he shared with those that made the mistake of trusting him. Adolescent Radar never seemed to know what was really going on and was much like the disciples who could never understand Jesus' parables and what they really meant. Then there were those that hung around as rank supporters, like Mary Magdalene who was sure to bolster the public opinion of Jesus' work about the same way as Hotlips kept the other M*A*S*H* women suspect to being equally promiscuous as she had been. Colonel Potter was the only stable one. His brain had to work overtime to compensate for all the other hair-brained problems that arose from his "disciples." Perhaps some of the calmer disciples felt this way too—that they had to play political clean up after Peter spoke, or Mary Magdalene was seen with Jesus, or when Jesus ate with the tax collectors.

The long-term view of His Army is that we're it, rag-tag and all. From the world's viewpoint we look like we've been thrown together with spare parts. We're weird, impetuous, inconsistent, and odd. We often come from the fringe of society to join this Army. We're the people most won't invite into their club. But, we were called, drafted, and enlisted into The Army of God. God, as the General of this Army, obviously has a sense of humor. Like Woody Allen, I too wonder "Do I really want to be a part of an organization that would accept me as a member?" But God's standard of using "the meek to confound the wise" has not been omitted in the structuring of His Army. Perhaps it is best seen here.

So when my brother or sister at church seems quirky or weird to me, I just grin. I know The General is still drafting all the rag-tags, the Hawkeyes and the Klingers. His TV commercials still remind us to "Be all that you can be… in the Army."

We Are the Army of God
Work Sheet

Theme: The Body of Christ
Day One: Read full essay.
Day Two: What is your view of the Army of God?

What part do you play in it?

_____

_____

What is the purpose of this Army?

_____

_____

Day Three: What historical pattern do you see in God's picking of this Army?

_____

_____

Why do you think this is?

_____

_____

Who is your favorite biblical Army draftee?

_____

_____

Why?

_____

Day Four: What strange people do you see in your own congregation?

_____

_____

What is their over-all purpose in this Army?

_____

How are they like you?

_____

_____

How are they different from you in positive ways?

_____

_____

Day Five: Who is your favorite current-day "odd" Christian hero?

_____

_____

What makes them odd?

_____

_____

How does this add to their success in this Army?

_____

_____

Day Six: What preconceptions did you bring to Christianity about "Christians"?

_____

_____

Has that changed?

_____

How?

_____

Day Seven: What criteria did Jesus use in selecting His Army?

_____

_____

Is that different today?

_____

How?

_____

Write a prayer blessing the oddest member of your congregational Army:

_____

_____

_____

(Note: Use extra sheets of paper, if required.)

"I Would Never Want To Be Part of an Organization..."

"...that would have me as a member." Woody Allen tells us this in one of his hilarious movies! I think he was quoting his friend Groucho Marx with that one. It was the 70's and my boyfriend and I were at the movies watching *Annie Hall* when I heard that line. I howled. We had gone to a 6-hour Woody Allen Film Festival where my need for eccentric humor was fed.

Woody is the neurotic kind of guy that you either understand **way** to well, or his humor doesn't even register with you and you only have a desire to beat him up. I'm obviously the kind of person that over-identified with him. His neurosis is the kind that the masses battle: inferiority, the need to be liked, feeling powerless and impotent, wanting to leave your mark on the world. With Woody, the moment people actually accept him, he then believes there is something wrong with **them**. It's a vicious cycle, which of course, has no solution.

I kind of felt that way about Christianity. On one hand, I was way too bad/wild/unholy to be part of the organization, and why would they want someone like me if they were trying to promote goodness? On the other hand, I was way too cool/chic/intellectual to be part of an organization that limited itself to the beliefs of one book. If "the organization" was inviting me in, which hand were they inviting, the bad/wild/unholy or the cool/chic/intellectual? I had not yet heard Billy Graham's theme song of "Just as I Am" to help me realize they were inviting both hands—both distorted perceptions of myself.

Once I was actually "in the organization" I found myself in good company. There were plenty of neurotics for me to identify with—Peter, Nebuchadnezzar, John the Baptist, Judas, Herod, and the wandering Jews, just to name a few. The longer I'm "in the organization" the more people I find to identify with, both in the Bible and in the pews. This was Jesus' way—the Body of Christ is a conglomeration of some odd ducks, but Christ, as the CEO of this organization, handpicked each one. He wanted each member in the organization. I remind myself that this even means Tele-evangelists, and like Groucho and Woody, I am part of an organization that wanted me as a member. I was weird enough to fit in—the bad/wild/unholy/cool/chic/intellectual. You are too. It's why Billy Graham reminds us each time He preaches to come "Just as I am." I can't help but think Woody needed to hear that too.

"I Would Never Want To Be Part of an Organization..."
Work Sheet

Theme: The Body of Christ

Day One: Read full essay.

Day Two: What personal characteristics did you initially think would keep you "out" of Christianity?

_____

_____

_____

_____

What made you change your mind?

_____

_____

_____

_____

Day Three: How has God used those very characteristics to the Body's benefit?

_____

_____

_____

_____

What did you initially believe about "becoming" a Christian as it related to these characteristics?

_____

_____

_____

Day Four: Are there any dichotomies between the characteristics you
bring to the Body? (Good vs. Bad) List them.

_____

_____

_____

Who do you identify with most in the Bible in relationship to the characteristics that you brought to the Body?

_____

_____

_____

Why?

_____

_____

_____

Day Five: Who do you think is the "oddest" person Christ chose to
be a disciple?

_____

_____

_____

_____

Why do you think He chose him?

_____

_____

_____

How did it turn out?

_____

_____

_____

_____

Day Six: What did the world teach you that kept you from coming
to the Lord earlier?

_____

_____

_____

How does the world view the Body?

_____

_____

_____

How does this compare to how you view it?

_____

_____

_____

Day Seven: How does your uniqueness compliment the Body?

_____

_____

_____

How does your uniqueness _not_ compliment the Body?

_____

_____

_____

How can the Body use your uniqueness best?

_____

_____

_____

How can you cooperate with this?

_____

_____

_____

(Note: Use extra sheets of paper, if required.)

He Uses the Simple Things to Confound the Wise

Tonight I got to hear Jake play the dulcimer and the cithara. He pulled up to the restaurant in some 1970's rattletrap, and drug his 6-foot-6 frame out of it leisurely. He walked stiff legged into the place, where he pulled up a stool, put out a basket and began playing the most angelic music this side of Dollywood and Heaven. He didn't stop to "work the crowd." He just sat down and strummed.

Jake always looks the same. In this day of rapid change, Jake is the constant. He always wears a short sleeve cotton tee shirt under a pair of huge overalls that are not buttoned on the sides. He comes vicariously close to showing us his Fruit of the Looms. His long 70's-type hair hangs loosely around his shoulders. His shoes look like they have as many miles on them as his car.

Jake is an anomaly. On one hand, he is considered "unusual"; on the other hand, he is truly a musical genius, a savant perhaps. He still lives with his mother on the family farmstead. I guess Jake started out in this world a little less "unusual" but has been hit by lightning three times and has lived. It wiped out part of his cognitive file on his personal computer, if you know what I mean. But perhaps it mysteriously downloaded some unbelievable musical megabytes onto his hard drive. This man plays all the old time long forgotten mountain instruments like the lap dulcimer, the saw, the mouth harp, banjo, cithara, the fiddle, and anything with a string. Of course, he's never had a lesson either. To help support his ailing mother, he plays around town for a price: a cold soda and the ability to lay a basket out. He invokes the angels of God to pull up a tree stump and tap their feet to "Amazing Grace," played on the saw and anything you can yell "Yee Haw" to!

Jake shares his faith through his music, playing at churches, or bars. It doesn't matter to him. Anywhere there is a stump to sit on, Jake shows up for the opportunity. With his non-church-like voice, He sings old mountain songs that would cause the Madonna to weep. He connects us back to our roots of church, Appalachian music where it all began, and a simpler time.

I count Jake as a modern day apostle. He's started plenty of churches in our hearts as we listened. He reminds us God is still in the miracle business, using simpletons to baffle us master degreed know-it-alls. I can see the Lord with a whimsical grin on His face watching us be blown over by the glory He reveals through the heart and gift of Jake. He confounds us after He has confronted our assumptions. Stuffed in those baggy overalls is some mighty fine talent brought here to jerk a knot in some "wise butt's" attitudes—like mine.

He Uses the Simple Things
to Confound the Wise
Work Sheet

Theme: The Body of Christ
Day One: Read full essay.
Day Two: What one "type" of Christian grips you the most?

_____

_____

_____

Why?

_____

_____

_____

Give an example of how this type of person has interacted with you:

_____

_____

_____

_____

Day Three: Name two ways this person is like you:

_____

_____

How would the Lord say they are like you?

_____

_____

Day Four: What gift do they bring to the Body?

_____

_____

_____

Do you see this person in a biblical character in the Bible?

_____

_____

What were the results in your biblical example?

_____

_____

Day Five: What prejudices do you still carry?

_____

_____

_____

Write a prayer asking God to remove these prejudices in you:

_____

_____

What have your prejudices done to the Body of Christ?

_____

_____

_____

Day Six: What have your prejudices done to your family?

_____

_____

_____

What would your kids say these prejudices have done?

_____

_____

_____

How does the world support your continuation of these prejudices?

_____

_____

_____

Day Seven: Research scripture about prejudices. What does it say?

_____

_____

_____

_____

_____

_____

How can you and the type of Christian that irritates you strengthen the Body of Christ together?

_____

_____

_____

_____

_____

_____

_____

(Note: Use extra sheets of paper, if required.)

Satan's Behaviors in Our Lives

The Exorcist and Rosemary's Baby portrayed Satan and the dark side of life in one particular manner. Sometimes he is gruesome and awful like that, but scripture reminds us that he was beautiful when he was in heaven and, even today, portrays himself as an Angel of Light. While we are waiting for Friday the 13th reruns in order to see the enemy at work, we might just miss him.

Some Christians still don't believe in Satan. I sort of envy their lives, in that they haven't gone toe-to-toe with him, but I know that only means "not yet." He is an active force in the physical and spiritual world. Our denial of his existence, unfortunately, doesn't stop his work upon the face of this earth. If we aren't looking for it, we darn might get blindsided by him; so the scripture reminds us to be wise and alert, looking for ways that he might hinder our lives. Scripture has not left us defenseless against him. If Christ lives inside of us, we have the tools with which to do battle against him.

Recently I did a youth lock-in, which is an "all-nighter" retreat. We were talking about the realities of Satan. Many children thought that Satan was a way their parents kept tabs on them and discouraged playful acting out. Most of them didn't know he was a real living being just as Christ is. I reminded the kids that if they were gonna play with Satan, that they might have the good manners to not get mad at him when he just does his job. His job has been to "steal, kill and destroy" (John 10:10), and it's still his job today; he hasn't been fired or demoted yet. That won't come until the end. So, until then, he's a force to be dealt with but not obsessed with. He will do his job; and he does a *good* job of stealing, killing and destroying.

Relationships, finances, marriages, spiritual development, character building, school, and children, are all game for him. He's up for all of it. One of our jobs as a Christian is to learn how he operates corporately in the life of the church and specifically in our lives. This is called Wisdom.

"Hello Mrs. Cleaver. You Sure Look Lovely Today."

I wasn't very old when Eddie Haskle was wooing Mrs. Cleaver in *Leave It To Beaver*, but I was old enough to sense a con artist at work. Slick Eddie was at work trying to get Mrs. Cleaver to believe some lie, overlook his character flaws, or let The Beav and Wally go off somewhere with him that they probably shouldn't go. But Eddie was moderately convincing because he looked all spit-shine clean and used a patronizingly convincing demeanor. He had his hair slicked down, his plaid shirt tucked into his creased pants, and shiny wing tipped shoes on. On the outside he looked pretty good. He counted on that approach. He radiated confidence when he complimented Mrs. Cleaver and had all the right words and smiles. Eddie, in little middle class suburbia, was the Angel of Light.

Isn't this how Satan operates in our lives? He tries to get us to believe some lie, overlook his character flaws or get us to go off somewhere we probably shouldn't go? He's moderately convincing because he looks all spit-shine clean and uses a convincing demeanor. Like Eddie, on the outside he looks pretty good and radiates a confidence when he is complimenting (and captivating) us into shooting ourselves right in the foot. The coy little smile and the sparkle in the eye are just enough to make us jump for the bait—right off the edge and over the cliff.

Jesus knows all about Satan looking good on the outside—the right looks, the right words—everything but the right motivation. He tried to clue the Pharisees in by giving them an analogy about a clean and dirty cup. The cup looked clean on the outside, like spit-shined Eddie, but on the inside it was dirty through wrong motivations—like Eddie. The world tends to judge the appearance of things—whether the cup **looks** clean, without really looking inside to see if it **is** clean.

"Hello Mrs. Cleaver. You Sure Look Lovely Today"
Work Sheet

Theme: Satan's Behavior in Our Lives

Day One: Read full essay.

Day Two: Do you have a sense of evil; can you discern it in others?

_____

_____

_____

_____

_____

_____

How do you know this?

_____

_____

_____

_____

_____

Describe an incident in which you felt it and then came to know what you felt was true.

_____

_____

_____

_____

_____

Day Three: List scriptures that describe Satan's character.

_____

_____

_____

_____

_____

Day Four: Take each description you listed about Satan's character and site an example in your life where you have seen it.

_____

_____

_____

_____

_____

_____

Day Five: Write a prayer asking the Lord to increase your discernment about Satan's operation in your life and the lives of those you love. Pray it all week.

_____

_____

_____

_____

_____

_____

Write down one area in which you think Satan is influencing your life today.

_____

_____

_____

_____

_____

_____

Day Six: Read the scripture about the clean and dirty cup. How is that true today?

_____

_____

_____

_____

_____

_____

What areas in your life look clean on the outside, but are dirty on the inside?

_____

_____

_____

_____

_____

_____

What proactive thing can you do about it?

_____

_____

_____

_____

_____

_____

To whom will you be accountable for changing this?

_____

_____

_____

_____

_____

Day Seven: Research scripture that tells you how to battle Satan according to God's plan (not our own). Write it here:

_____

_____

_____

_____

Write it on an index card and put it in your Bible where you can have easy access to it.

Use it daily. Putting on the Armor of God should be part of the beginning of your prayer life every day (Ephesians 6:11). You should pray this before launching into any other kind of prayer.

(Note: Use extra sheets of paper, if required.)

Who's Afraid of the Big Bad Wolf?

We all were afraid at sometime of a big, bad-breathed wolf. After all, he had the power to dismantle houses and lives and send pigs squealing in fear. He warranted our respectful fear as children but are we living the same way today, as adults? Do we give Satan our respectful fear?

Jesus tells us we don't have to live in fear of him. He is subject to us if we are subject to Christ. In other words, the wolf must leave if the pigs say so. Very often we don't bother to say "Go"—we stay huddled in the corner hoping he will just go away.

In 1997 a battle raged for my family. In the beginning I did not notice it as a battle; but as houses were blown down, lives messed up and family members went running in fear, it suddenly occurred to me that maybe Satan was dismantling my homestead for some reason. By the time I realized it every one was in such bad shape from it, that there were no immediate family members to stand in battle with me. Friends bellied up to the altar for me and prayed for most of that year. The battle, however, was not turning yet. The family village was still on fire; our lives were still smoldering. I was too weary to think and now my health was failing from stress. I would like to think that my next action was a spiritual decision, but I think it was a survival tactic. I threw all my favorite books in the trunk of my car, a Bible, a pad of paper for writing and a sweatshirt. I drove from Florida to a cabin in North Carolina where I used to pray. I didn't call ahead. I just showed up.

For the next five days, the Lord took over. I don't remember much except that the Lord drew me into deep intercessory prayer every few hours, for days. When it was over, the wolf was gone and the family village was saved from complete ravage, I noticed that prayer brought my village back from the brink of destruction. Prayer brought me back too.

I don't fear the Big Bad Wolf like I use to. I'm a smart pig now. I know how to tell him to "Go!" He can huff and puff but he ain't blowing this joint down!

Who's Afraid of the Big Bad Wolf?
Work Sheet

Theme: Satan's Behavior in Our Lives
Day One: Read full essay.
Day Two: Why do you fear Satan?

_____

_____

_____

_____

_____

_____

List specific things he has done to you or your family.

_____

_____

_____

_____

_____

Day Three: Research scripture to see how Jesus dealt with Satan. What did you learn?

_____

_____

_____

_____

_____

How can you use that?

_____

_____

_____

_____

Day Four: Write a prayer and ask God to teach you what you need to know about Satan.

_____

_____

_____

_____

What specific thing do you fear most about Satan in your life, or the life of your family?

_____

_____

_____

_____

Pray about that now. Use the Armor of God (Ephesians 6:10–18).

Day Five: Research your favorite Bible character and list all the ways you saw Satan at work in his/her life.

_____

_____

_____

_____

Do any of those apply to you?

_____

_____

_____

_____

How did the Bible character deal with Satan?

_____

_____

_____

_____

_____

Can you apply that to your life?

_____

_____

_____

_____

_____

Day Six: Ask your best friend or Pastor if they see Satan active in your life.

Talk openly about it. Hear what they have to say. Have them pray with you about it.

Day Seven: Go to a Christian Bookstore and find a book about how to battle Satan and begin reading it. It will change your life and the lives of those whom you pray for. Write your commitment here as to how you will promise to battle Satan for yourself or your loved ones:

_____

_____

_____

_____

_____

_____

_____

_____

_____

(Note: Use extra sheets of paper, if required.)

The Wizard of Oz

The big head belching smoke yells, "I am the great and powerful Oz." He's scary enough to frighten a teenager, a sissy lion, a scarecrow and a tin man. Only the little dog Toto was brave enough to expose the Oz for what he really was…a little old impotent man. The curtain is pulled back and truth is revealed. The image on the screen is a lie. He isn't big and scary and powerful. "Don't mind the little man behind the curtain!" Oz says, tryng to cover the revealed truth.

I love this metaphor. I used it a lot in counseling. Satan does this in our lives. He portrays something bigger than life on a screen— belching smoke, yelling and screaming, trying to terrorize those that are weak in spirit. But if the curtain is pulled back, we see a little old man at a control board frantically trying to cover up the real story. Satan too knows the real story. He even knows the end of the story when he loses. That's why he works so hard at the illusion and projection on the screen now. He's on borrowed time. If he's gonna get any satisfaction at scaring sissy lions, scare crows and tin men, now's the time to do it. He's just a talking head; the picture of all un-respected authority. But now is not the time to forget Toto, just a little dog, exposed his weakness! Just an attempt at reaching at the truth showed what was really behind the curtain.

What a weenie, an old man trying to feel powerful at the expense of others! How is he any different from Satan? And like Dorothy, we have every right to get angry and yell, "Why, you are nothing but an old man!" Hit him where it hurts, Dot! "You should be ashamed of yourself" she taunts. (This we know Satan never feels, but nonetheless…) With this newfound truth, the frightened five find fury; their anger fuels them to fight back, not with fear but with truth!

The yellow brick road that we are following might not lead us to Oz, but the lessons can be valuable to us anywhere we travel.

The Wizard of Oz
Work Sheet

Theme: Satan's Behavior in Our Lives

Day One: Read full essay.

Day Two: How do you see that Satan is a "false front" like the head in Oz?

_____

_____

_____

_____

_____

How does he blow smoke in your life today?

_____

_____

_____

_____

Day Three: What did you fear most about Satan when you were little?

_____

_____

_____

_____

What do you fear most about Satan as an adult?

_____

_____

_____

_____

How have these two fears changed?

_____
_____
_____
_____
_____

Day Four: What is the biggest truth you know about Satan?

_____
_____
_____
_____
_____
_____

How can this truth empower you to fear less?

_____
_____
_____
_____
_____

Day Five: How can you temper fear with wisdom when it comes to Satan?

_____
_____
_____
_____
_____

What things do you need to truly fear and what things do you need to be wise about?

_____
_____
_____
_____
_____

Discuss these with someone who is a mentor in the spiritual faith.

Day Six: Satan's job is to steal, kill and destroy.
What is he stealing in your life?

_____

_____

_____

_____

What is he destroying?

_____

_____

_____

_____

What will you do to push the battle line back?

_____

_____

_____

_____

Day Seven: What area in your life are you probably ignoring, that Satan wants to get his hands into?

_____

_____

_____

_____

_____

Become accountable to someone else for working this area of your life, so Satan does not enter.
What things do you need to renounce in your life that Satan may be using?

_____

_____

_____

_____

Pray a prayer of renouncement with someone.
(Note: Use extra sheets of paper, if required.)

Salvation and Faith

This is the nitty-gritty. The core, the stuff, or as my friend Toni would say, "the funk" is why we gather together, why we are radical enough to call our selves "Christian." This is why you picked up this book in the first place because you have either swam out in the deep end or you're thinking about it. Either way, welcome to the 'hood.

Salvation and Faith are an anomaly. You've gotta have one to have the other; but sometimes it feels like you haven't got either one. Many are surprised to find out they have both! Salvation is the beginning; it's a gate, a doorway, a ladder, and an entrance. Faith is the end…it's a gate, a doorway, a ladder, and an entrance. The combination of Salvation and Faith is like seeing the end from the beginning and the beginning from the end. The cool thing about Christianity is that you get to do that! You see the beginning of your faith as you accept Christ, the beginning of your learning and growing in Christ and the beginning of your Salvation-walk; but you also get to see the end now! How cool is that? The Bible shows us the outcome of our Salvation-walk. It shows us what comes after this gig. It shows us how it all ends, and what comes next. It tells us how the new world will look and what we will do there. You get to see your life from end to end!

It's trippy to be able to see your life, through the eyes of Salvation as the beginning, and Faith as the end. The hard part is all the living that has to go on between those two bookends. Sometimes when life gets hard, I think that I have all the answers if God would just listen.

Don't you? Life gets squirrelly, and walking out this Salvation thing gets hard. Waiting in faith for tomorrow, much less eternity, can feel overwhelming or even scary. But don't fear, there IS someone steering this "Magical Mystery Bus." and it isn't The Beatles. He's called the Holy Spirit and rumor has it, He's a pretty good cabbie.

Ladies and Gentlemen, please make sure your seatbelt is securely fastened. We are about to depart.

If I Were the Boss of the Circus

Dr. Seuss books like *If I Ran the Circus* were my favorite books as a child. The truth is, I still love them and have kept them all these years. How do you grow up without *Whoville* or *The Cat in the Hat*? I was rearranging my bookshelf recently when I saw my Seuss books. The one that caught my eye was *If I Ran the Circus*. I chuckled at the thought of our lives as a circus with God as the Ring Master.

Haven't you had the thought that God hasn't run His circus well at times? I have. You don't get very far into the Book of Genesis before you think "Uh, oh…not a good idea." There isn't a woman alive that agrees with God's plan for pregnancy, fertility, or menopause, based on the error in the Garden. Men don't think "toiling the land" for the Garden screw up was a good idea either. And what was God thinking when Satan was created? Satan makes a good antagonist in a plot line, but He isn't much fun to really live with. If the Jews were my people, I wouldn't waste time by letting them walk in circles for forty years. I wouldn't have picked Peter, Judas, or Mary Magdalene to hang around with. I would have done away with mental retardation, schizophrenia and cancer. This is what I would do if I ran the circus.

If I look at the circus I have run I think, *"I haven't run it very well either."* I don't make the best Ring Master myself. The choices I made in high school, the end of my previous marriage, failures with my children, my moodiness…I have run a circus and this is what I got!

God has a plan for His circus too. It included His child hanging on a tree to save degenerates. I wouldn't have done that if I ran the circus. It's a good thing The Ring Master does!

If I Were the Boss of the Circus
Work Sheet

Theme: Satan's Behaviors in Our Lives

Day One: Read full essay.

Day Two: Are there times that you have thought God hasn't run the circus well?

_____

_____

_____

_____

Why?

_____

_____

_____

What has happened in your life that seemed, at that time, like it wasn't a good plan by God?

_____

_____

_____

_____

Day Three: How has that plan changed your life from when it first happened?

_____

_____

_____

How has God used that plan over time?

_____

_____

_____

Has He been able to use it in others' lives as well?

_____

_____

_____

Do you think it will be able to be used later in someone's life?

_____

_____

_____

Why?

_____

_____

_____

Day Four: How are you hoping in faith He will use it?

_____

_____

_____

How are you hoping in faith you will use it?

_____

_____

_____

How do you see this playing out?

_____

_____

_____

Day Five: How has God run your circus well?

_____

_____

_____

What specifically has He done that has worked out well in your life?

_____

_____

_____

How has He used that for His Glory?

_____

_____

_____

Day Six: How has He used that to help others?

_____

_____

_____

_____

What is God's plan for us?

_____

_____

_____

Research scripture and find six things God says about His creation:

_____

_____

_____

What did you learn about what God said?

_____

_____

_____

Day Seven: Write a prayer asking God to help you trust Him more, in faith, for the outcome of your life:

_____

_____

_____

_____

Write on a Post-It the words "More Faith" and put it somewhere you can view it all month long.

Who do you know who has wonderful faith that you would like to imitate?

_____

_____

_____

Why?

_____

_____

_____

(Note: Use extra sheets of paper, if required.)

"It's Froggy Out, Mommy"
(My daughter Lindsay at age 3)

This morning as I write, the fog is thick and heavy and fills the whole cow pasture, from the top of the cove to the ground; visibility, about to the end of my yard. When Lindsay was little, she called it being "froggy" outside. It reminds me of old Dracula movies where the "fog rolled in on the bog." It's an every day occurrence here as it pours over the Blue Ridge Mountains each morning. Driving in it on curvy mountain roads can be scary.

Fog has a way of making it appear that there is nothing beyond what you can see. From here, I can see 10 feet into my yard but in reality, there is 25 acres beyond that. I know a lot of people who operate in life that way. The fog in their life has made it appear that the only reality is what they see 10 feet ahead of them. But let's face it, if we're driving in fog we're driving by faith that the road is beyond what we see or we wouldn't dare to drive at all. There's also lots of things beyond the fog of our lives if we drive in faith, and we only realize the road is really there if we keep moving ahead.

Our visibility can be obscured by more than just fog. The fog in our lives can be lots of things—unbelief, skepticism, distorted thinking, lack of faith, or negativity. It clouds the roadways of our lives with a heaviness we can't see through. It makes us believe there is nothing beyond the 10 feet we can see. That, in itself, is pretty limiting. I've got to have more than 10 feet of space in my life and in my faith. If we don't believe there is anything beyond the 10 feet, we don't just operate cautiously; we end up operating in fear. We operate out of the assumption that what we can't see isn't real.

The weather type of fog will dissipate; the fog of our lives is our choice. People that I know that operate their lives out of the "fog in the bog" have a very concrete view of life—dispelling that anything exists beyond what they see or think that they know. In a concrete world-view, there is no place to put something as abstract as faith. Faith is something unseen.

Fog impairs our visibility of faith—faith in God, love, hope and possibility. It keeps us glued to the driveway of our lives without rolling forward to see what is on the other side.

Turn your low beams on!

"It's Froggy Out, Mommy"
Work Sheet

Theme: Salvation and Faith

Day One: Read full essay.

Day Two: What is obscuring your faith? List all the things that are standing in the way of a deepening faith:

_____

_____

_____

_____

How do you think this came about?

_____

_____

_____

What are you most concerned about?

_____

_____

_____

Day Three: Write a prayer and ask the Lord to show you how to deal with the things that are standing in the way of a deepening faith:

_____

_____

_____

_____

_____

Write down anything He tells you about this:

_____
_____
_____

Discuss this entire issue with your accountability partner.
Day Four: Whose faith do you admire?

_____
_____
_____
_____

Why?

_____
_____
_____
_____

What is the strongest thing about their faith?

_____
_____
_____
_____

How can you incorporate that in your life?

_____
_____
_____
_____

Day Five: Lifestyle choices can also negatively affect our faith. What
in your lifestyle needs to change?

_____
_____
_____
_____
_____
_____

How will you change this?

_____

_____

_____

_____

Day Six: A lack of time in the Word will also negatively affect our faith. How much time do you spend in the Word?

_____

_____

_____

_____

How much time do you need to spend in the Word to produce positive movement in your faith?

_____

_____

_____

_____

Discuss this with your accountability partner.

Day Seven: What would happen in your life if your faith radically expanded?

_____

_____

_____

_____

Write ten things you think would happen:

_____

_____

_____

_____

_____

(Note: Use extra sheets of paper, if required.)

Two All-Beef Patties, Special Sauce, Lettuce, Cheese, Pickle, Onion On A Sesame Seed Bun™
(McDonald's Corporation Jingle)

Remember it? Say it really fast. McDonalds hypnotized us with this little diddy years ago. It was McDonalds' first really unique commercial that lured us in. It became legendary.

Christianity isn't exempt in this category either. As I write this, The Prayer of Jabez is big, but I know I will survive, because I've lived thru a lot of other Christian commercialism equal to the two-all-beef-patties gig. I remember the Name It and Claim It that was big in the Bakker hay day and the Inner-Healing workshops. How about the Faith-Only Movement, the advent of Christian self-help, the spiciness of the Deliverance Movement, or the emotionality of the Charismatic Renewal? I remember the big focus on signs and wonders. Now we have the whole Left Behind series that gives new thought (and fear) to Eschatology. I even have friends that are following this gold dust thing that is supposed to be appearing on people.

We might poo-poo the commercialism of Nike, Pierre Cardin or the mall, but we're just as hooked. When life gets boring we head to the mall, when church gets boring we head to the scriptures for a new twist. We tweak them just a bit to get something new...something that cranks our prayer fuel at the altar. We aren't any different than the Israelites that whined about manna getting boring. Jesus just gets plain manna-ish. It's milk-toast, it's hamburger helper night after night, it's an O'Douls™ beer without the kick.

I don't take much of it to heart. "Being blown by every wind of doctrine" however, ends up meaning "for someone else," when people get way too hyped up on some little commercial diddy. I remind them of this scripture, but of course, they never feel it's for them. I end up being just some ol' stick in the mud when it comes to a "fresh movement of God." I know their shopping at the scripture mall, but I also know they'll be back. I just hum the commercial while I wait... "Two-all-beef-patties-special-sauce-lettuce-cheese-pickles-onions-on-a-sesame-seed-bun.™" I'll take a diet coke with it...to go.

Two All Beef Patties
Work Sheet

Theme: Salvation and Faith
Day One: Read full essay.
Day Two: What Christian gimmicks have you lived through?

_____
_____
_____
_____

How do you feel about them?

_____
_____
_____

What effect have they had on you, your faith or your walk?

_____
_____

Day Three: What would Christ say about a lot of the gimmicks that have passed through the doors of the church?

_____
_____
_____
_____
_____

How does He bring balance to those gimmicks?

_____

_____

Day Four: Do you have the type of personality that tends to get caught
up in gimmicks; whether from the 70's, 80's or in Christianity?

_____

_____

_____

If so, why?

_____

_____

What did you get caught up in during those eras?

_____

_____

_____

If you didn't, why not?

_____

_____

_____

Day Five: How can you keep the Lord exciting in your life so that you
don't tend to search out the gimmicks to do it?

_____

_____

_____

What will you commit to doing to keep Him exciting?

_____

_____

_____

Day Six: Talk to a Christian friend today about gimmicks.
What do they say about it?

_____

_____

_____

_____

How do you think these things affect Christianity?

_____

_____

_____

Day Seven: If you don't go for the gimmicks, does that mean you are
   boring?

_____

_____

_____

Does it mean you have a lack of faith?

_____

_____

_____

Does it mean you are "missing God?"

_____

_____

_____

What does it mean?

_____

_____

_____

(Note: Use extra sheets of paper, if required.)

Hold 'Em, Fold 'Em, Walk & Run

To paraphrase Kenny Rogers in the song from *The Gambler*, you gotta figure out when its cool to hold 'em, when it's more cool to fold 'em up, when you gotta walk away from something and when the heck to run—Kenny's only quoting Jesus here—did ya know that? Jesus said to dust off your sandals and move on when people had been given the truth and refused it.

Sometimes we equate evangelism with steer wrestling. We grab them by the horns, wrestle them to the ground, brand them with a burned cross on their leg, and won't let them up till they cry Jesus—or Uncle! Then we are aghast when people think Christians are pushy and uncivilized. We've been in the saddle so long we've lost our manners! We've had too much cowboying and not enough curtseying. Too much scripture slinging gets as bad as breathing on someone with whiskey-breath. We can get downright obnoxious.

Didn't the very wise C. S. Lewis say, "Christians are the best and worst case for Christianity"? Perhaps our hostage-taking evangelism tactics proved this point to C. S.

I am all for evangelism, especially the kind that Jesus did. He strolled into to town and developed relationships through preaching, healing or helping. Bingo! Converts! Some of those that did most of the evangelism in the early centuries learned this too. In the 12th century when Christianity was spreading rapidly despite gnostic humanism, St. Francis of Assisi did the same thing…"Preach always, if necessary, use words" he told his men.

Lighten up! Christians don't need to be known by the adage "They don't make friends, they take hostages!"

Hold 'Em, Fold 'Em, Walk & Run
Work Sheet

Theme: Salvation and Faith

Day One: Read full essay.

Day Two: What is your overall view of evangelism and salvation?

_____

_____

_____

_____

_____

Give supporting scripture for that viewpoint:

_____

_____

_____

_____

Day Three: How do you think Christianity, overall, handles evangelism?

_____

_____

_____

_____

Why?

_____

_____

_____

_____

Day Four: List three things you have seen someone doing in evangelism that you did not like:

_____

_____

_____

_____

What would Jesus say about those things?

_____

_____

_____

Support that with scripture here:

_____

_____

_____

Day Five: What one awful thing have you done that you wish you hadn't, in talking to someone about Christ?

_____

_____

_____

_____

Did it have a negative outcome for you or the person you were talking to?

_____

_____

_____

_____

Why do you regret this?

_____

_____

_____

_____

Day Six: What do you do if you see a Christian being "inappropriate" while talking to other people?

_____

_____

_____

_____

What will you do?

_____

_____

_____

_____

What should you do?

_____

_____

_____

_____

What does Christ say to do?

_____

_____

_____

_____

Day Seven: How did Jesus evangelize?

_____

_____

_____

_____

Give five examples here:

_____

_____

_____

_____

_____

List how you will incorporate these into your own approach to evangelism:

_____

_____

_____

_____

(Note: Use extra sheets of paper, if required.)

Blowing in the Wind

B ob tells us answers are blowing around in the wind, but I don't think so. Bob Dylan sings it so believably! Feel free to chase those leaves blowing down your driveway. Pick one up and turn it over. See if any meaningful answer is written on. Is there? No. I didn't think so.

Rock and Roll told us the answer was in a lot of places. This was the most benign—"in the wind." Most of us thought it was in a bong or a bottle. Even Dylan tells us that the answers are out there blowing in the wind for us to grab. But even though we are older, and hopefully wiser, the world is still telling us the answer is somewhere else; in money, in success, in careers, in notoriety, in stuff, in technology, in multiple relationships, in crazy types of non-descript religions, in our bodies, and even in our own divinity. It keeps us chasing after a lot of blowing wind and leaves looking for something that is never there.

In the book of Ecclesiastes we are reminded to stop chasing the wind. Now this guy had it going on! He isn't misdirecting people to follow a mass of air they can't see. He isn't telling them to get out in the middle of the wind and be blown around in a small hurricane. He knows darn well if you are out seeking answers in the wind you're gonna get an eyeful of dirt. Standing in a wind tunnel at an amusement park isn't likely to blow answers into your head. But we do that, don't we? We dial psychic lines or listen to our psycho friends. We read magazine articles that promise to fix our lives. We do the same thing over and over again and expect it to be different.

The book of Ecclesiastes tells us the truth that the world won't tell us. It tells us that chasing the wind isn't any smarter than chasing our tails. If you are chasing the wind, how do you know when you've caught it? I think the only way you know you're facing off with the wind is when you get that eyeful of dirt. Now, how smart is that?

Blowing in the Wind
Work Sheet

Theme: Salvation and Faith
Day One: Read full essay.
Day Two: Where does the world tell you the answer is?

_____

_____

_____

_____

In the past, where have you tried to find it?

_____

_____

_____

_____

How has any of that carried forward in your life today?

_____

_____

_____

_____

Do you sometimes revert back and try to find it somewhere else?

_____

_____

_____

_____

Day Three: When Christianity is distorted, where do you sometimes hear that you can "also" find the answer?

_____

_____

_____

_____

What do you think about that?

_____

_____

_____

_____

What does Christ say?

_____

_____

_____

_____

Day Four: List four scriptures on Truth:

_____

_____

_____

_____

_____

How does Christ describe Himself when it comes to being the answer?

_____

_____

_____

_____

List the scriptures here:

_____

_____

_____

_____

Day Five: What are you chasing that you should let go of now?

_____

_____

_____

_____

Write a prayer asking God to help you let go of it:

_____

_____

_____

_____

Tell your accountability partner about it.

Day Six: Listen closely, all day, to the conversations of everyone you talk with. List all the things in which they are looking for the answer:

_____

_____

_____

_____

_____

What did you learn?

_____

_____

_____

_____

Any surprises?

_____

_____

_____

_____

_____

Day Seven: Repeat Day Six.

_____

_____

_____

_____

_____

_____

_____

(Note: Use extra sheets of paper, if required.)

Super(Duper)Natural

Perfectly normal Christians don't believe in the Supernatural. Can you believe that? I would like to be inside their head for two seconds to see how they rationalize that a Supernatural God did not create the world Supernaturally or does not continue to operate in the Supernatural now. I don't get it! These same perfectly normal Christians are the ones who call the Psychic Hotlines and check their Horoscopes. They believe in the supernatural when it comes to mere mortals, but not when it comes to the great I AM. David Copperfield even has a chance with them to get them to say, "That was a miracle." But they don't consider the creation of the world, the incarnation, or the resurrection to be "miracles" because they don't believe them. Please, someone whack me up side the head! This is too much!

Do you really think a psychic living in a trailer has more answers for you than the God who created the inner workings of something so complicated as an eyeball? If that psychic knows so much, didn't she know she would end up living in a trailer and using food stamps? Ditch the National Enquirer Horoscope page and open up the Bible if you want to see Supernatural; or better yet, just watch real life. Every day miracles occur that are not aired on daytime talk TV or emergency rescue shows. Every day people defy death that doctors said was imminent. Babies are born healthy, despite ultrasounds that claim doom and gloom. People walk, see, and are healed every day by the power of Grace and Mercy. Money comes in from an unknown source to a family who has prayed for supernatural intervention so they don't lose their house. A child is found. Relationships are mended.

I sorta pity people who don't believe in the Supernatural. Too bad, it's cool stuff. I'm glad I have a cool God that still does mind-blowin' events on a daily basis. A friend of mine from my Bible college days taught me something very wise; it probably changed how I looked at and for God. She said, "Look and expect to find a miracle a day;" then every night at 7 P.M., I had to call and report to her what I found. I did this for almost three years. I've never been the same since...

Manic Mysteries

Mysteries are cool, and Christianity is full of them. If you're not intrigued by mysteries at heart, then Christianity isn't for you. I can't name the Seven Wonders of the World but I can tell you they aren't cooler than the mysteries of Christianity. How 'bout that incarnation, a couple of resurrections or "missing off the face of the earth" stuff? Who can explain stigmata, walking on water, parting water and covering the earth with water…who has repeated that? What Wall Street financial nerd can explain why tithing works? How about the physics of things changing from their original forms: water into wine, Jesus walking thru walls, the many healings where people regained sight or limbs? How cool is a talking donkey? What 'bout raising a dead man? Seen any manna lately at the 7/11? And—even cooler unexplainables are yet to come, according to the Book of Revelation.

There aren't any trippier stories than the ones you read in scripture. Scripture is jam-packed with full color adventure, rich in *The Outer Limits* type stories. Christians should never be bored for a lack of a good story line. Anywhere you open the book there is some unexplainable, some "outer limit" example of God's own type of physics and science.

I think we either don't really believe all the stories in scripture, or we become numb to them after so many years of hearing them. We shouldn't—instead we should let the stories shift us into awe, where we begin to hear them with new ears. How can we yawn through the incarnation or count the mints in the bottom of our purse during walking on water? These are extraordinary! Even in a Steven King fiction movie, you aren't gonna get anything like this! This is the real thing, the big cohune, the O-rig-a-nal. People flock to sci-fi movies but church sermons should be just as rich—full of outrageous/never-again-seen wonders.

This Sunday when you hear "Lazarus come forth!" belted from the pulpit, stop doodling on your bulletin and hear the mystery!

Manic Mysteries
Work Sheet

Theme: Salvation and Faith

Day One: Read full essay.

Day Two: Find a "Miracle Seeker Partner" for the next two weeks. Look for God's hand at work every day in your life; call your Partner at a predetermined time each evening and share what you saw. Let them tell you what they saw God do for them. Write your miracle here:

_____
_____
_____
_____
_____
_____
_____
_____

Day Three: Repeat

_____
_____
_____
_____
_____
_____
_____
_____
_____
_____

Day Four: Repeat

_____
_____
_____
_____
_____
_____

Day Five: Yep! Repeat

_____
_____
_____
_____
_____

Day Six: Repeat

_____
_____
_____
_____
_____

Day Seven: You're in the groove. Repeat

_____
_____
_____
_____
_____

What have you learned this week?

_____
_____
_____

(Note: Use extra sheets of paper, if required.)

Now I Only See a Dim Reflection in a Mirror, One Day I Will See "Face to Face"
(1 Corinthians 13:12)

This seems like an important thing for me to remember. It's a wake up call about our innate lack of insight and discernment of spiritual things. This is definitely something that I struggle with. I get so caught up in the day-to-day-ness of my life that I rush by the spiritual implications. When I am too busy, my life turns only physical. The spiritual realm seems to fade to "dim." If I am running short of money this month, it's because of something extra we purchased. It's not because we perhaps skipped a tithe or there is something else spiritual going on in our lives (or not going on!). It gets really scary when I miss something going on with my kids because I am too wrapped up in the physical world. The physical world isn't going to give me discernment about what my kids might be doing.

I don't like that I fade in and out of "seeing" the spiritual side of things when I get too busy. But even with our fading in and out of spiritual reality, Jesus promises us that one day we will see "face to face." All our one-dimensional-ness will be shed like an old snakeskin and we will "see"—really see—what life was about; the other dimension behind everything that always existed. It will be like a two-way mirror. We will look through the mirror and see what is really happening. I could sure use that two-way mirror while I am still on this earth. Anyone with teenagers **wants** a two-way mirror!

The scripture found in the title of this essay helps me to come back to the spiritual dimension when I've wandered too far and taken my physical life way too seriously. This isn't all there is, and it isn't all there will be. On the other side of the mirror, cool stuff is happening and being prepared. Every once in a while, run your hand over the glass of the mirror…and wave!

now I Only See a Dim Reflection in a mirror, One Day I Will See "face to face"
Work Sheet

Theme: Salvation and Faith

Day One: Read full essay.

Day Two: Continue this week with your Miracle Seeker Partner. Look for God's Hand at work every day in your life and call your Partner at a predetermined time each evening and share what you saw. Let them tell you what they saw God do for them. Write your miracle here:

_____

_____

_____

_____

_____

Day Three: Repeat

_____

_____

_____

_____

_____

_____

Day Four: Isn't it cool? Repeat

_____

_____

_____

_____

Day Five: Mind blowing, eh? Repeat

_____

_____

_____

_____

Day Six: Repeat

_____

_____

_____

_____

Day Seven: Repeat

_____

_____

_____

_____

What have you learned about God over the past two weeks that you did not know before?

_____

_____

_____

_____

_____

In what ways have you learned to see Him that was different than before?

_____

_____

_____

_____

_____

How can you share this with others?

_____

_____

_____

(Note: Use extra sheets of paper, if required.)

Mental Health

Each theme that is covered in this book has meaning to our spiritual formation and development. Each theme contributes to our development into the likeness of Christ. Some themes, I feel, have significant implications as to how well we will develop, and can even be seen as warning signs for developmental pot holes in our journey. As a Christian counselor I, of course, have seen how people's mental health has significantly impaired their ability to grow emotionally and spiritually. I have seen denial in national ministries destroy the evangelist or pastor as they refuse to get help or allow others to guide them in the process of restoration. I have seen Christ misrepresented as someone who would oppose good mental health when, in fact, He is our example of all that is mentally healthy! I have seen God used as some genie whose lamp can be rubbed, resulting in our problems evaporating, based on a single prayer. All of this keeps us from being all that we can be for Him, and prevents us from being used by Him in something that is healthy and that outlives our own meager lives.

We all come to the pew with significant baggage because we live in a world that has been wrecked by sin. Sin in and of itself produces baggage; so none of us are immune. We just need to lug that thing in, throw it on the pew with us, and let God help us sort through it. He knows what's in there anyway and there isn't anything in there that will surprise Him. He's just waiting to help us sort it. The more we try to deny that we own a big piece of baggage, the more the thing haunts us. We need to stop judging each other for baggage. Blame it on sin, that's where it started anyway! We're just human and frail and responding to sin in all its awfulness. But there is a way through it and on the other side is some groovy living waiting for you! You have a Brother who will walk with you through it and a Father who will help you sort. It's just a big old pile of dirty laundry. Yes, it smells to high heaven, but it's bleachable. So just get started…

"You Can't Be a Contemplative If..."

"...you don't own a cat," according to George Carlin, a heathenistic comic of the 60's/70's. George learned something of enjoying the moment by watching his cats. Animals do have a way of teaching us the fundamentals of life, and even perhaps, the fundamentals of the gospel.

St. Gabriel is my all-white-pushing-20-pounds cat. He has the personality of Gandhi and is a peacemaker among the woodland critters that live on my mountain. He was also used as a "therapeutic pet" at my counseling center years ago. He's older than Moses and also wiser, as he hasn't spent 40 years wandering to find his Promised Land. Gabe has learned his Promised Land is *right here, right now.*

Gabe has *never* panicked (except with a thermometer at the vet's office). He doesn't worry about food, what he'll do today or where he will take his fifth nap of the day. He doesn't counter attack when birds dive bomb him or squirrels tell him off. He never loses his serenity.

Our two large Akita dogs may try to chase him but Gabe has learned that when a 130 pound animal wants to "chase" you, it's best to just lie down with your belly up and declare it all over with. The dogs can't chase a drop-dead, still cat.

Gabe doesn't fight about food either. When bossy Sophia the kitten hogs all the food, Gabe takes two steps backwards and sits, waiting in faith that there will still be some for him when she's done. Gabriel is always rewarded for his faith; there is always food left. If Sophia wants the softest chair for her nap, Gabe just totters over and lies down somewhere else, knowing his needs for a nap will be accommodated as easily in a different location.

Gabriel has learned some gospel truths better than a few humans I know. He has learned to not worry—about anything—ever (except the thermometer!) The only place the Holy Spirit exists is in the present moment. He was with us in the past and will be with us in the future, when we get there; but for this moment—*right here, right now* is where He is. One way to miss feeling His presence is by worrying…money, relationships, bills, car repairs, kids. Jesus reminded us to not worry today. Jesus knows worry will be there tomorrow when we awake, but He tells us the lilies of the field don't even bother to worry. The birds don't bother to worry. Nature is obviously smarter than we are; it bows to the Creator and all the needs are met. He reminds us that we are more important to Him than lilies and birds. That's His guarantee of taking care of us. He only asks that we "cast our cares on Him."

Gabe has cast a few cares away too, and he's a lot happier for it. Gabe and Sophia are curled up for nap #5 on the porch. The sun is streaming in, a small breeze blows, a few birds chirp from deep in the woods. I think I will just sit here and contemplate them a few minutes and see what else they can teach me. For today, they remind me that life is good.

"You Can't Be A Contemplative If ..."
Work Sheet

Theme: Mental Health

Day One: Read full essay.

Day Two: Go some place quiet. Sit quietly. Do not listen to anything. Notice how busy your mind is. Just notice. See what types of things you worry about. Just notice.

Go home. Write down what you worry about.

_____

_____

_____

_____

_____

_____

Just for today, do not watch TV or listen to the radio.

Day Three: Review your list of worries. Are they worthy of your
time?

_____

_____

_____

_____

_____

Do you get solutions from worrying?

_____

_____

_____

_____

Why do you do what doesn't work?

_____

_____

_____

_____

What will you do differently?

_____

_____

_____

_____

Do it.

Just for today, do not watch TV or listen to the radio.

Day Four: Go some place quiet. Sit quietly. Do not listen to anything.
Notice how busy your mind is. Just notice. See what types of things
you worry about. Just notice.

Go home. Write down what you worry about.

_____

_____

_____

_____

Write a prayer asking God to help you release the worries.

_____

_____

_____

_____

_____

_____

Just for today, do not watch TV or listen to the radio.

Day Five: Get in a warm bathtub. Do not listen to anything. Just focus on how good the warm bath is feeling. Let all your awareness go to the one issue of feeling the bath.

Just for today, do not watch TV or listen to the radio.

Day Six: Watch the sunrise or the sunset. Do not listen to anything, just focus on watching the beauty unfold. Let all your awareness be focused on that one issue of watching the beauty. Just for today, do not watch TV or listen to the radio.

Day Seven: Get in bed with your favorite book. Do not listen to anything. Just focus on the joy of resting and reading. Let all your awareness be focused on that one issue of resting and reading. Just for today, do not watch TV or listen to the radio.

Write down how your week has been as you have watched no TV, listened to no radio and learned to turn your focus to one thing at a time:

_____

_____

_____

_____

_____

How could this change your life?

_____

_____

_____

_____

(Note: Use extra sheets of paper, if required.)

"DANGER! Danger, Will Robinson!"

The Robot from *Lost in Space* whirls his metal arms around wildly as a warning. If you are a clueless person in a strange land, a mouthy robot is a good thing to have. Will didn't have to analyze his choices very deeply because the robot would always tell him when he had made a bad enough choice that was leading him into danger. Perhaps the evil alien was approaching or some other unidentified person—"Danger!" the robot would yell and flare his accordion arms.

I am a clueless person in a strange land and I need something more in-tune than myself to tell me when the evil alien is approaching too. Do you feel that way? Will Robinson wasn't the only person living in an alien environment. The scripture reminds us that once we have accepted Christ, this is no longer our home. We become nomadic in spirit-sort of wandering along until we get to go to our true home. It is why it is so hard to be comfortable in this world after Christ lives in us.

Nonetheless we are here in a land that now feels strange, and our job is to maneuver through it. The evil alien is here too, waiting to broadside someone who didn't read the clues of his impending attack. I could use the robot flailing about when I am just about to really screw things up.

We have something more effective than the robot to warn us of our choices. The Lord did not leave us defenseless in an alien world. In fact, prior to His crucifixion He told His disciples He would have to leave but He would send someone who would be with them always. He sent the third part of the Trinity—the Holy Spirit. The Holy Spirit's job is to help us live in an alien world. He's our holy translator. **He translates the world's real motives into warnings for us.** He's a little different from the robot—he doesn't flail and shout, He is "still" and has a "small voice." We don't get an obvious robotic stop sign, but we do get instructions from the translator if we will listen.

"DANGER! Danger, Will Robinson!"
Work Sheet

Theme: Mental Health
Day One: Read full essay.
Day Two: Do you realize when you are about to make a bad choice?

_____

_____

_____

_____

How do you know?

_____

_____

_____

Does your body tell you in some way?

_____

_____

_____

Does your conscience tell you in some way?

_____

_____

_____

Day Three: What does your culture teach about making choices?

_____

_____

_____

What does your culture teach about making bad choices?

_____

_____

_____

What did Jesus teach on this subject?

_____

_____

_____

Day Four: What skills do you have to maneuver through this alien world?

_____

_____

_____

What extra skills does the Bible offer that you don't have?

_____

_____

_____

What Bible character can you relate to when it has to do with choices?

_____

_____

_____

_____

Why?

_____

_____

_____

Day Five: How does the Holy Spirit warn you about danger?

_____

_____

_____

_____

If you perceive that the Holy Spirit does not warn you when you are about to enter into danger, write a prayer right now asking the Holy Spirit to show you and guide you away from danger.

_____

_____

_____

_____

Day Six: Do you hear the "still small voice"?

_____
_____
_____
_____

How do you hear it?

_____
_____
_____
_____

When do you hear it?

_____
_____
_____
_____

What do you do when you hear it?

_____
_____
_____
_____

How should that change?

_____
_____
_____
_____

Day Seven: If you do not hear the "still small voice" contact your accountability partner today and continue to pray with them that you will learn to hear the "still small voice".

Make quiet time every morning prior to any activity to sit quietly. Don't even read.

Just listen.

Rearrange your schedule to make time to "listen." Hearing precedes decision-making.

(Note: Use extra sheets of paper, if required.)

Let the Dead Bury Their Own
(Jesus)

This morning as I am trying to enjoy the chill of the air, my morning is being interrupted by our newest distraction—Chance, the 75-pound, 6-month old Akita puppy. At 75 pounds, the only thing that really qualifies him as a puppy is his stupidity. Chance enters insanity every morning. That clashes with my peak of writing creativity, which also happens to be in the morning. He runs in circles, trots like a filly, pulls down clay pots as they smash on the patio, finds a pair of socks to drag through the mud, chases a hummingbird, pulls a chunk out of my wicker table and then to his delight, finds a dead baby mole.

I find this quite a metaphor: moles are blind and destructive and Chance is stupid and destructive. He finds a dead friend and alerts me to it. Akita's are hunters so, of course, he wouldn't let the mole just be dead. He tried to go about his morning ritual of combing the woods on the upper tier but he kept running back to the mole, distracted by it's deadness. He runs and gets his ball, drops it and runs back to the mole. I keep yelling for him to leave it alone. I go to get more coffee and when I return, of course, the mole is gone and I see Chance running like a colt with a dead mole bouncing from his lips. My stomach does a big roll and I put on my flip-flops to chase him and the mole.

Flip-flops put me at a distinct disadvantage in cornering this mini-race horse. The look on my face (the death-stare) convinces him to drop it. I scoop it up in a bag and throw it in the outside garbage can. Chance is now sitting guard in front of the cans.

Chance isn't any more stupid than some of us who also find fascination in dead things that were blind to begin with. We carry around and/or guard dead things as if there is still life in them. In counseling, we call this "baggage"; but I think a dead, blind mole is a better image. We keep carrying around the destructive rodent as if it will one day become something more than it is. We nudge it to see if it's "still" dead. Yep, it is. And we pick it back up. We lay it down and sit guard over it.

Our dead mole may be a mindset, a way of not relating, a situation we refuse to make right, a belief, or an entire way of life. Chance's fascination is obviously fueled by its deadness; us too. We just don't think it's because it's dead-we just keep hoping it will turn into something. We aren't living Cinderella's life where mice become horses and pumpkins become carriages. We live where dead moles are dead moles.

The Bible tells us to let the dead bury his own. **Whoa!** What a confrontation. Since no mother mole showed up to bury this baby, I did it, but what about you? For your own sake, bury that mole! It really is dead.

Let the Dead Bury Their Own
Work Sheet

Theme: Mental Health
Day One: Read full essay.
Day Two: What dead thing are you carrying around?

_____
_____
_____
_____
_____
_____

How long has it been dead?

_____
_____
_____
_____

What is blocking you from burying it?

_____
_____
_____

Day Three: What would God say you are carrying around?

_____
_____
_____
_____

How would He tell you to go about burying it?

_____
_____
_____
_____

When will you do it?

_____
_____
_____

Day Four: Give the most predominant aspect of Jesus' mental
   health:
How can you imitate that in your life?

_____
_____
_____
_____

What one thing in your life really needs professional advice?

_____
_____
_____
_____

When will you do it?

_____
_____
_____

Day Five: What has your culture taught about the concept of counseling?

_____

_____

_____

_____

What has Christianity taught about the concept of professional counseling?

_____

_____

_____

_____

Does this bar you from seeking help if you want it/need it?

_____

_____

_____

What type of groups have you tried?

_____

_____

_____

Would you try one again?

_____

_____

_____

Day Six: Research scripture on counseling/seeking advice.
What predominant theme did you notice?

_____

_____

_____

How can you apply that in your life?

_____

_____

_____

What Bible character motivates you to face this in your own life?

_____

_____

Day Seven: What thing from childhood are you still carrying?

_____

_____

Write a prayer and ask God to show you what He wants you to do about it.

_____

_____

_____

_____

What thing from your teen years are you still carrying?

_____

_____

Write a prayer and ask God to show you what He wants you to do about it.

_____

_____

_____

What thing are you still carrying from adulthood?

_____

_____

_____

Write a prayer and ask God to show you what He wants you to do about it.

_____

_____

_____

Then do it.
(Note: Use extra sheets of paper, if required.)

The Immaculate Reception
(A Freudian-Slip, By Ken Brown)

The Immaculate—are we discussing the Virgin here? No, we are just discussing Martha Stewart. No magical virgin stuff, but most certainly, an immaculate something or other at Martha's house; and of course as always, a reception that her instruction will make even more perfect than you had already busted your butt for.

Did I ever tell you how Martha single-handedly ruined my life? In my 30's when developmentally women are prone to "want" to do things homey and entertaining, I took Martha seriously. It was a deadly error. I watched her re-runs until I could recite them like a mantra. Then, I believed I could do all those things without her staff, run a counseling ministry, go to school, be married, raise two kids and write a book. Why not? Martha trims her whole grove of trees in an hour show?

Especially habit forming was anything that had to do with Christmas. Living in Florida then, I always had the propensity of overdoing things because it never really felt like Christmas there. This year, Martha suggested putting trees in all your rooms. Forget Advent Calendars-we were living an Advent Progressive Decorating Calendar. It took one month to decorate our house, provided we put up some decorations every night. There were two live trees; one in the family room decorated in country and one in the living room decorated in Victorian, with all hand made ornaments from suggestions by—you guessed it, Martha! Then there were artificial trees in the rest of the house: One in the entry way with a mish-mash of no themed ornaments and the nativity set below it; one in the dining room done in gold; one in the master bedroom done in hearts; one in the kitchen done in horns (in the memory of my dad who was a trumpet player); one in the guest potty on the back of the toilet; one in the hallway upstairs outside the kids bedroom that was their little tree that they decorated with handmade things from school. Outside was garland and big red bows that covered the white picket fence. Christmas lights were on the front of the house. Inside the house, my children were laying on the floor each and every night crying, begging not to have to do this night after night. Then there was the night we had to hang wreathes on the doors, in the windows, on the inside doors and greenery over all the doors and on the top of cabinets. —More crying and even trying to hide in their rooms.

Tra-la-la-la-la, does any one want some eggnog? Oh, we have got to plan the ministry Christmas party here at the house so everyone can enjoy the trees in every room. —More crying (ungrateful kids). Remind me to pick up the color coordinated matching wrapping paper so it doesn't clash with the tree. What night do you want to make the homemade bows for the packages? I can't believe the kids don't want to make homemade Christmas cookies this year. What's wrong with them? Kids get the Christmas cards out and help me address them. This pile is for the ministry, this is for relatives, and this is for friends…use the right kind of stamps too. Tomorrow night we will decorate homemade stockings, ok? What do you mean you don't feel like it? (Ungrateful kids!) Every night it's the same thing, your stomach hurts! This weekend it's pictures with Santa; so don't plan anything! "All I want for Christmas is Prozac" Lindsay says.

The Immaculate Reception
Work Sheet

Theme: Mental Health
Day One: Read full essay.
Day Two: List five things you think you "might" be unbalanced with
    in your life:

_____

_____

_____

List five things your kids would say you are unbalanced in:

_____
_____
_____
_____
_____

Which are true?

_____
_____
_____

Day Three: What types of things do you worry about?

_____
_____
_____
_____

Why?

_____
_____
_____

Research scriptures on worry and anxiety.
What did you learn?

_____
_____
_____
_____

Day Four: What did Jesus have to say about worry/anxiety?

_____
_____
_____

What Bible character do you see as worried?

_____
_____
_____

Which one do you see as compulsive?

_____

_____

_____

How did these defects affect their lives?

_____

_____

_____

Day Five: What you worry about says a lot about you. What does it say about you?

_____

_____

_____

_____

What does culture teach us about worry?

_____

_____

_____

_____

How does that compare/contrast to what the scripture teaches?

_____

_____

_____

What are you currently doing about your worry/anxiety/compulsions?

_____

_____

_____

Day Six: Name three ways your compulsions have spilled over into other people's lives:

_____

_____

_____

_____

_____

How do you feel about that?

_____
_____
_____
_____

What are you willing to do about that?

_____
_____
_____
_____

What would Jesus advise you to do?

_____
_____
_____
_____

Day Seven: Call an accountability partner, pastor or counselor and
    discuss these aspects of your personality.
List a plan for addressing these in your life:

_____
_____
_____
_____
_____

Find a group for it. Go to it.
Write a prayer asking God to help you with these areas of your per-
    sonality and life:

_____
_____
_____
_____
_____

(Note: Use extra sheets of paper, if required.)

Family

What's the old saying, "Family is where they *have* to take you in?" Since the onslaught of self-help, that probably isn't true any more as families "set boundaries" and perhaps close doors on bad behavior. But Christianity is another family where more than likely; they will take you in. It's the Christian heritage that we take all the wayward, prostitutes, throwaways, politicians, and Capitol Hill degenerates. If they don't want you, Jesus said, you will always find an open door in our community...and family. Even if we don't really want you, we will still probably take you in. So, we live by Jesus' example that always kept options open for those that were hurting and lost. Eternity was always offered and available. A new life, in a new family, would always be waiting when they "found their way home."

Family is broad and expansive. That means our biologics...those we are under one roof with and born into, as well as our spiritlogics... those that we are joined to in the spirit realm once we have accepted Christ. Our family gets **really** big once we accept Christ. Sure, the potentiality for a Jerry Springer™ Breakout probably exists when you get that many people to gather under the name of Christianity.

We've got to learn how to do this thing—this Christian Family thing. Jesus showed us how to care for people, reach out, disciple them, set limits for them, and point them heavenward. We've also got to learn how to be Jesus to our own biologics. Day in and day out we have to demonstrate Jesus to our kids, parents and even the weird relative we don't like. There's some humor in all this. There's got to be when you put this many people together! So look for the humor in your own family! It's there! (Just don't call Jerry Springer with it.) Also look for it in the **really** big family all across the world.

Don't get all hung up on the genealogy of all this or the genetics of it either. After all, we've all got an awesome bloodline!

Question: How Many Pairs of Sunglasses Does It Take To Be Happy? Answer: None.
(By Ken Brown, my husband)

My husband was recently telling a story about being in Wal-Mart and "feeling like buying." He looked at tee shirts, then a VCR and finally picked up a pair of $10 sunglasses, even though he had a pair propped on his head. He carried them around the store as he perused other options. He aborted right before check out, putting the glasses back on the rack and walking rapidly to the exit. "Why?" I asked. "I was restless. I was trying to make it go away. So I asked myself how many pairs of sunglasses does it take to be happy and the answer was clear. It wasn't the source of my restlessness and it wouldn't be the source of my happiness...so I left." WOW! This was MY husband having this profound insight!

Jesus told us to "store up your treasures in Heaven where neither moth nor rust will decay it." He was showing us where to invest our money and ourselves. He shows us it is not in "stuff" but in investments that Heaven deems valuable. What does Heaven value? It values things like a godly character, healthy family relationships, acts of charity and assistance, prayer, tithing, and joy. I guess Ken looked around Wal-Mart and didn't find any prayer, charity or other items worthy of investment.

"So what did you do?" I asked. "I invested it wisely. I took our daughter to lunch and spent time with her." Taco Bell turned out to be The Road to Less Restlessness.

Question: "How many tacos does it take to be happy?"

Answer: "Just a couple with your daughter."

Question: How Many Pairs of Sunglasses Does It Take To Be Happy?
Work Sheet

Theme: Family
Day One: Read full essay.
Day Two: Where is your treasure?

_____
_____
_____
_____
_____

Ok, now really, where is it?

_____
_____
_____
_____

Where would your kids say it is?

_____
_____
_____
_____

Where would your partner say it is?

_____
_____
_____

Day Three: Where does most of your time go?

_____
_____
_____
_____

Make a chart here:

What did you learn?

_____
_____
_____
_____

Day Four: What do you want to value?

_____
_____
_____
_____

What do you want to invest in, that you currently are not?

_____
_____
_____
_____

How can you make this happen?

_____
_____
_____
_____

Day Five: Write a prayer asking God to show you where you are investing and where He would like for you to invest:

_____
_____
_____
_____
_____

Share this with your accountability partner.

Day Six: What does the Lord value? List it here (must be scriptural):

_____

_____

_____

Which of these do you value?

_____

_____

_____

Does your life show that you value these?

_____

_____

_____

Day Seven: Which of these do you think is really important that you work on?

_____

_____

_____

How will you do that? List your plan here:

_____

_____

_____

Ask your children what they think you should work on:

_____

_____

_____

Which will you work on now?

_____

_____

_____

(Note: Use extra sheets of paper, if required.)

He Puts the Lonely in Families
(Psalm 68:6)

Last night I was digging in the garden when our friend Jimmy called. He lives half the year in Arizona and was just making it back; four months later than usual. He had gone back to "tie the knot." Jimmy had dated the woman for seven years, after the death of his wife who was manic-depressive. I had heard that something went very wrong and he didn't get married. We had been waiting four months for this call to find out exactly what had happened.

Jimmy, who has a heart the size of Dallas, is also mentally ill. He battles his own brain chemistry and on good days, with low stress, he functions well. Spiritually he functions better than most of us—directing food banks, always helping others, housing homeless with him… doing whatever he can. He never says no, and errs on the side of generosity, even if others use him.

Jimmy's ancient truck bounced down our gravel driveway. His head was shaven nearly bald and he looked old and worn. I knew the last four months weren't good ones. He got out of the truck and hugged my husband. He was thin, unshaven and mildly disoriented. He sat on a stack of logs smoking cigarettes and recounting what went wrong. He had gone out to marry Cindy. But five days before the wedding; a woman he had worked with over the past four years, who is very mentally ill and drug addicted, told him she had feelings for him. Many people would have said, "I'm sorry but I am in a committed relationship," but for Jimmy it turned his world upside down. The brakes screeched, the marriage was halted and Jimmy spent four months "exploring" this other relationship, to his own demise.

Linda led him down a road of constant chaos, mind games, drinking and drugging (despite his years of sobriety) until Jimmy lost his internal compass of which way was God. He ended up in a psych ward and was released only because he promised to leave the area and come back to North Carolina. Now, confused, he wonders "when" Linda will get well enough to be in a relationship with him. With her extensive diagnosis, I know the answer is probably "never" and I know when Jimmy will want to hear that is probably "never." There are just some mental illnesses that are never successful in relationships; and she has one of them.

Jimmy went on to say that all his relationships had been with mentally ill women. We talked for hours. After a plate of shrimp and a cup of coffee, I was sure we were no further ahead. He was headed back to Arizona to sell his house and live full time here; but I felt reasonably certain he would go back, hook up with her and end up in the psych unit again.

Jimmy's old truck meandered up the drive with some counseling books I gave him on the seat of it, so he could "understand" her diagnosis. I tossed and turned all night in bed, waking for only moments to pray for Jimmy, that God would protect him as he couldn't protect himself. My husband called it "kind" that I spent hours talking with Jimmy about this. But this scripture, Psalm 68:6, came to mind and that God puts Jimmy's in our families because families give a sense of emotional and spiritual strength. Families are His design—designed as a fortress when life's battering is too much. When that happens we find refuge in the arms of our family. Jimmy kept saying he had no family in Arizona and that might have been why he crashed on the shores of bad choices. The whole Body of Christ is our family—a place of strength and refuge. Jimmy is given to us that we might practice being the arms of Abba, as a living family of God.

He Puts the Lonely in families
Work Sheet

Theme: Family
Day One: Read full essay.
Day Two: What has the world taught you about the issue of family?

_____

_____

_____

How is the world's view and the scriptural view different?

_____

_____

_____

What has your past taught you about reaching out to others?

_____

_____

_____

Day Three: Was your family one that reached out to others?

_____

_____

_____

What did your family think of the "poor in spirit" or others who needed help?

_____

_____

_____

How has that translated to your current view of this population?

_____

_____

_____

Day Four: How should the Body of Christ be family to others?

_____

_____

How did Christ demonstrate this for us?

_____

_____

_____

How far do we go?

_____

_____

_____

Are there any limits? If so, list them with scripture references:

_____

_____

_____

Day Five: Write a prayer asking God to give you a heart for the sense of "family" within the Body of Christ. Write what He tells you about this:

_____

_____

_____

_____

Find five scriptures and list them here about family:

_____

_____

_____

What did you learn?

_____

_____

_____

_____

Day Six: Today serve someone in the Body of Christ.
Write about it here:

_____

_____

_____

_____

How did you feel?

_____

_____

_____

_____

Day Seven: Repeat Day Six
What did you learn?

_____

_____

_____

_____

_____

_____

_____

_____

How is your concept of family changing?

_____

_____

_____

(Note: Use extra sheets of paper, if required.)

We Are Fam-I-Lee

Than in the itself is a miracle. If you have

T his weekend, my husband and I had a mini-vacation with our girls, now almost 21 and 17. This in itself is a miracle. If you have teens and young adults you know they would rather appear in public in totally nerdy clothes than to be seen with their parents. So, the fact that they "willingly" wanted to go on a vacation with us, shocked us into unadulterated happiness; and leeriness too… "Why would they want to go with us—and what are they going to pull?"

My almost 21-year-old, Lindsay, now lives on her own; so going on vacation with us was going to be odd for both of us, after all, if she acts up in the car, it is unlikely we will turn around and pop her one. By the sheer act of her living by herself, it changed our roles a bit on this vacation. Lauren, at 17, hasn't quite shed the whinny complaining-ness of a teen…you know, the kind that can cause angels to contemplate cursing. So cramming the four of us in Lauren's Toyota for six hours each way was going to test the bonds of this family-thing.

Now every vacation traveling family knows the mystical dynamics of vacation destinations: you are irritated by the constant question of "Are we there yet?" but basically the kids don't fight much. Every vacation traveling family also knows the mystical dynamics of vacation returns: you are irritated by the constant fighting of the kids all the way home, as the anticipation of fun is no longer a motivation for good behavior. Well, this is also true for 21 and 17 year olds. Traveling to our destination, the kids slept and chatted and worked word puzzles. On the way back Lauren was yelling that Lindsay was picking lint off of her flannel pillowcase and throwing it on her velvet car seats. (*Never* go on vacation in one of your children's cars. If necessary, steal a car and risk going to jail, but *never* take your child's car.) To irritate her further, Lindsay took her pillowcase and rubbed it up and down on the seats. Lauren, in retaliation, immediately took off her gym shoes and socks and rubbed her athlete's foot on Lindsay's bare arm as she reminded her it was contagious. Lindsay, who doesn't even weigh 100 pounds, grabbed Lauren's stomach area and asked, "Do you want some butter with this roll?" Lauren, having sat on the side of the car that was getting pounding heat all day, grabbed Lindsay's face and pulled it into her armpit for a whiff.

Meanwhile, Lauren is telling Ken he is driving her car all wrong. He needs to drive faster, use the blinker, go thru the car wash, and buy this type of gas. Ken too is now wondering why he didn't risk going to jail by stealing a car…

In the hotel room, here is family at it's best…nostalgic memories that waif through like an aroma…the girls curled together asleep in a double bed…elbows flailing in the night, legs wrapped around each other, the sleepy sounds of sisters. I smile with great remembrance…I hear a sleepy statement, "Sister, move over." How sweet, I think. "I'm gonna knock you out…" she replies. Ahhh, yes indeed, "we are fam-i-lee."

We Are Fam-I-Lee
Work Sheet

Theme: Family
Day One: Read full essay.
Day Two: What did Jesus teach us about the concept of family now and in eternity?

_____

_____

_____

_____

How can you apply that today?

_____

_____

_____

_____

What might you have to lay down in order for this concept to really take hold in you?

_____

_____

_____

_____

_____

What makes you uncomfortable about this?

_____

_____

_____

_____

_____

Day Three: Write the funniest story about your own biological family:

_____

_____

_____

_____

_____

List three of your family's strengths as you were growing up:

_____

_____

_____

_____

Day Four: Write the funniest story about your own children:

_____

_____

_____

_____

_____

List three of your family's strengths today:

_____

_____

_____

_____

Day Five: Write the most inspiring story about your family when you were small:

_____

_____

_____

_____

_____

_____

_____

List three weaknesses your family had back then:

_____

_____

_____

_____

Do you see them in your family now?

_____

_____

_____

_____

_____

_____

Day Six: Write the most inspiring story about your family now:

_____

_____

_____

_____

_____

List three weaknesses your family has now:

_____

_____

_____

_____

What are you committed to doing about these as a family?

_____

_____

_____

_____

Day Seven: Write a story about your current family in the future…five years from now. Describe your life then.

_____

_____

_____

_____

Now come back to REALITY, how can some of that be now?

_____

_____

_____

_____

Write a prayer here asking the Lord to consecrate your family to Him:

_____

_____

_____

_____

_____

Believe that He will do it now!
(Note: Use extra sheets of paper, if required.)

Charity and Service

Now here's a mind blower, eh? Serving others! Yep, vacating the couch and serving meals to the homeless, weather proofing the homes of the elderly, or painting the walls at a domestic violence shelter. How about delivering groceries to a food bank, organizing a team of visitors for the hospital, or mowing the grass of a gay neighbor whose mower is broken? Yes, I said gay.

Trippy concept, huh? It has all the makings of a science fiction movie, doesn't it? But some of us think this because by the time we were growing up, charity and service were old concepts not being regularly and radically practiced. Mothers were going to work for the first time and time was a premium so out went helping others, volunteering, and church attending. These were all frivolities that a two-income family could no longer "enjoy." So many of us were raised watching The Salvation Army do what ordinary people use to do—what all of us who were "civil, kindhearted Americans" did. So, finding our way back to service and giving is awkward and we must remember why we are doing this—a reason beyond our own magnanimous sense of "giving to those less fortunate."

We do it because Jesus said it was an important spiritual principle and formational tool in our lives. God is the ultimate recycler. He uses everything at least twice. So, as we serve someone else it does something in those whom we serve, but it also does something in us as we serve. It even does something in those who watch us serve. Serving and giving, forces our heart to be soft and supple. It untangles the kinks in our worldview that thinks everyone is living how we live. It challenges our own subconscious prejudices about certain types of people, the cycle of poverty and even our theology about God's Will in the calamities of life.

It rattles our cage, cranks our choke, presses our buttons, and pushes our limits...Good! We need it. We go home and we see our own luxuries, we see our wastefulness, we see our attitudes. Worse yet, we see the next generation living these attitudes in our children. We wonder how far we have come...because we were the ones who supported MLK, JR, fought racism, or spent time raising conscientiousness about AIDS or women's issues. We were the front-liners at one time, before time and giving became a luxury we could no longer afford. Then we sat on the sidelines of humanity and watched the world unravel and felt fragmented from a process we once created.

So, this is why we do it. Because when we give out of our own brokenness, we see something of Christ in our selves and in those who are broken that we give to. We see the brotherhood of Christ in both of us, which unites us. Jesus told us, "Whatever you have done to the least of these, you have done unto me." Christ is among the poor and the broken, the elderly and the sick, watching to see if we stoop to hold His hand, or lift Him up. And when we do, recycling is birthed, in me, in you, in them.

The Great Use of Life is to Spend it for Something That Outlasts It
(William James)

I spent today with someone new I met. Her name is Ruth. I was startled when I met her, as she only has about three hairs on her head. She has had chemotherapy that was ineffective. She weighs less than a hundred pounds and she is dying of lung cancer. As she lit a cigarette she told me she was shocked to be dying. "I am only 59" she said. I was there to help her get more services along with what hospice will provide.

On my schedule for next week is to go meet Lillie who is also dying of cancer. It's been a sad week: A Hospice Service of Remembrance for all who died in Hospice this year, meeting Ruth and knowing I will meet Lillie. It was time to ask the unanswerable question, "Why is death so ugly, God?"

The hospice nurses have told me about "beautiful deaths." which I would like to see, where people of faith die with smiles and faces radiant with the expectation of the Lord.

I could use seeing one of those types of deaths about now. Each person that I work with that begins to die, makes me wonder if they feel like they have fulfilled what they were put here for. Have they spent their lives on something bigger than themselves? More importantly, have they spent their lives on something that will out live them? Scripture admonishes us to live our lives in this way. Everything rots and turns to dust except what we have done "unto the Lord." Only love is eternal and outlives us. Only serving God through love is an investment that lives beyond our own gravestone.

Last week I went to see Mr. Potts who is 92 years old. I asked him what he needed and with great sincerity he said, "More time." Acts of love, acts of service, or acts of benevolence reminds us that we have the capacity to outlive our names. We have the capacity to invest in eternal stocks and bonds that dust will not decay.

Next week is Lillie, a dear older African American woman whom I will find out from whether she is ready for this journey or not. I might just meet the radiant face that has lived her life for something bigger than herself.

The Great Use of Life is to Spend it for Something That Will Outlast It
Work Sheet

Theme: Charity and Service

Day One: Read full essay.

Day Two: Research scriptures about what we are suppose to invest in that outlasts us. List those findings here:

_____

_____

_____

_____

_____

How are you doing in regard to investing in those kinds of things in your life?

_____

_____

_____

_____

_____

What can you do differently?

_____

_____

_____

Day Three: Give three Old Testament examples of someone investing in something that outlived them:

_____
_____
_____
_____
_____

What did you learn?

_____
_____
_____
_____

How can you apply that?

_____
_____
_____
_____

Day Four: What needs to occur in your ego so that this can continue to be an easy way of natural thinking and living?

_____
_____
_____
_____

How did the Lord demonstrate investing in something that outlived Him physically?

_____
_____
_____
_____

Write a prayer asking the Lord to help you do this:

_____
_____
_____
_____

Day Five: What person do you know that seems to do this effort-
lessly?

_____

_____

_____

_____

_____

How do they demonstrate this?

_____

_____

_____

Why does this have meaning for you?

_____

_____

_____

_____

How is the person like you?

_____

_____

_____

How is the person different than you?

_____

_____

_____

Day Six: What acts of charity and service that you have done, do you
hope live on past you?

_____

_____

_____

_____

What are you most proud of?

_____

_____

_____

_____

What are you least proud of or ashamed of?

_____

_____

_____

_____

What do you want to do in charity and service?

_____

_____

_____

_____

Why?

_____

_____

_____

_____

Day Seven: Do something today. Write about it here:

_____

_____

_____

_____

_____

_____

(Note: Use extra sheets of paper, if required.)

Green Acres
(From the TV series Green Acres)

When I moved here, my friend Rick teased me about being too "foofy" to move to the mountains. He said that I was like Lisa from *Green Acres* and that I would be out riding a tractor in a feather boa yelling, "Oh, dahling....Oh, O-lee-va..." Well, that was hardly true and he has since, personally seen me in my overalls here on the mountain. I live in western North Carolina and find that what I really love most is "small town living." It's the life for me!

The other day I was in a small independently owned pharmacy. It really serves us "socially" as an old general store—as people congregate long after they've gotten their medicine to talk about births, canning, revivals, who is "a ailin'," and crops. Prayer needs are exchanged. And there is a lot of "rejoicing with those who rejoice and mourning with those that mourn," going on at what is commonly referred to as "Steve's."

Steve helped me out when a 36-year-old patient of mine was dying with brain cancer. She was "rounding the corner" as we call it, and in pain. Her dad got scared in the middle of the night and called Steve at 2 A.M. Steve went to the pharmacy and compounded a special drug to help her deal with the pain until she "rounded the corner." He delivered it to the home where she comfortably died in the wee hours of the morning.

Steve knows everyone and dispenses more than medicine—some neighborliness goes out the door with every bagful of tonics. "How's that youngin' Edith?" He yells. "Joe, did ya get that engine runnin'? No? Here call my friend, he'll hep ya." "Beulah, is Buster still a ailin'? Take this to him...No, No, I can't charge ya for it." "Ain't that the purtiest baby I've ever kissed?"

"Here's your medicine Russell. Is it doing well for ya?"

"No, doc. I'm still a hurtin'."

"Lets call your doctor right now and ask him if you can take more than one a day." Steve calls the doctor and they chat.

"Ok, Russell, he says it's ok to go to twice a day." Russell doesn't respond for a while. Then he whispers, "But if I do, who will feed me? I can't afford both…"

"Ah…Russell, come by my house today and we'll have some supper and I'll load you up with some groceries. Here's your medicine. Now, you're coming 'bout six, right?"

Russell grins, "Yup, if the Lawd's willin' and the creek don't rise."

Russell and Steve both laugh.

Christianity 101 just demonstrated. Did ya'll take notes?

Green Acres
Work Sheet

Theme: Charity and Service

Day One: Read full essay.

Day Two: Name ten aspects of charity or service in Christianity.

_____

_____

_____

_____

Which are you most comfortable with?

_____

_____

_____

Which are you least comfortable with?

_____

_____

_____

_____

Why?

_____

_____

_____

Day Three: How did Christ demonstrate charity and service?

_____

_____

_____

How did the disciples demonstrate this?

_____

_____

_____

How did biblical characters in the Old Testament demonstrate this?

_____

_____

_____

Day Four: Whom do you see demonstrating this?

_____

_____

_____

What does your congregation do to demonstrate this?

_____

_____

What does your community do to demonstrate this?

_____

_____

_____

What needs to be done that isn't being done?

_____

_____

_____

Day Five: Tell your accountability partner one aspect of charity or
service you are willing to do in the next month. (Cannot be simply
giving money, must be "doing" something) List it here:

_____

_____

_____

_____

_____

What issues stirred you when you were younger?

_____

_____

_____

What did you do in charity or service about those issues?

_____

_____

_____

Day Six: What issues stir you now?

_____

_____

_____

Are they different than the issues from when you were younger?

_____

_____

_____

What cultural influencing have you picked up about charity and service?

_____

_____

_____

_____

What cultural influencing have you picked up about your issue?

_____

_____

_____

_____

Day Seven: Why do you think being involved in charity and service is important for your growth?

_____

_____

_____

_____

_____

What is the purpose of doing something for others?

_____

_____

_____

_____

What is a biblical principle that you get from that?

_____

_____

_____

_____

How can Christ be manifested in these situations for you?

_____

_____

_____

_____

(Note: Use extra sheets of paper, if required.)

He Ain't Heavy, He's My Bro...

The Hollies, in the 70's song "He Ain't Heavy, He's my Brother" and Jesus both remind us to lend a hand, a heart, a buck or a truck to someone in need. It's not hard to do, just stand still with your eyes open and you will see someone who could use something. Here's the hard part—then do it!

A sack of groceries here, a ride there, a listening ear, a kind word, an arm around a shoulder, a hearty laugh together, a bowl of soup, two good and useful books, $10 bucks in the kitty, a prayer, six smiles, a box of towels and blankets, a loaf of home made bread, a phone call with no agenda, a visit to the nursing home, a thoughtful card.

Pick one for today and one for tomorrow. Pretty soon you will have a habit. I didn't realize this until a patient and friend was in a nursing home. I went to see her and took her some tulips from my yard, a bottle of lotion and a picture of my dog, Molly, whom she loves. I asked her if she wanted some books. "No, I am very busy right now, but the best gift of all is that you came to see me. I can't tell you how wonderful that is!"

Two days later, she was busy dying. My tulips sat at her bedside heralding her death.

Make time. Waiting two days might be too late to help a brother carry a heavy burden.

He Ain't Heavy, He's My Bro...
Work Sheet

Theme: Charity and Service
Day One: Read full essay.
Day Two: How do you tend to help others?

_____

_____

_____

_____

How do you balance codependency (doing for others what they can do
    for themselves) with bearing one another's burdens?

_____

_____

_____

_____

Describe the difference, as you see it:

_____

_____

_____

_____

Day Three: How do you determine a need?

_____

_____

_____

_____

Do you assume need?

_____

_____

_____

Do you ask someone about his/her need?

_____

_____

_____

Ask one person about a need today.

_____

_____

_____

Day Four: How do you feel when other's needs are met and yours are
not?

_____

_____

_____

_____

How do you get your self outside of that, so that you can be less focused on yourself?

_____

_____

_____

_____

Do you over focus on other's needs and ignore your own?

_____

_____

_____

_____

How can you balance in this?

_____

_____

_____

Day Five: Ask two people about a need today. Describe what you did
or are going to do about it:

_____

_____

_____

_____

How do you feel about meeting this need?

_____

_____

_____

_____

Day Six: What has God blessed you with that will allow you to meet other people's needs in certain areas?

_____

_____

_____

_____

As a child, in what ways did you attempt to help other children?

_____

_____

_____

_____

Is that similar to how you help as an adult?

_____

_____

_____

_____

Day Seven: Name three people who come to mind that you can assist:

_____

_____

_____

_____

Write a prayer for each person asking God to not only meet their need now, but help them to have their needs met in the future:

_____

_____

_____

_____

(Note: Use extra sheets of paper, if required.)

All You Need Is Love, Love, and More Love

We believed it in the 60's when John, Paul, George & Ringo sang "All You Need Is Love". We chanted it like a mantra. We took our bras off to prove it (why did we think that proved anything?). I wonder why we don't believe it now. We actually believe it less now, even though Jesus has been declaring it for 2000 years.

The Beatles never really did define what this "Love" was that we all needed. We all came to understand it as Free Love/Communes/Out of Control Behavior. Jesus had already defined love for us; and it turns out to be diametrically opposed to what St. John, St. Paul, St. George and St. Ringo said it was. We don't have to run through "Strawberry Fields" to find it, live in a "Yellow Submarine" or become "The Walrus" to experience it.

Jesus described love with a lot of adjectives in the Book of Corinthians. You know it well…"*Love is patient, kind, non-boastful.*" etc. But He also went on to describe love as a verb; action, living and doing. "*When you have **done** this unto the least of these, you have **done** it unto me.*" "*It is better to **give** than receive.*" When you see someone in need…

The Beatles were right in theory "all we need is love" if our love has feet, hands, and motion; if we put something behind love that propels it forward. If not, then we risk what Paul of the Gospels (not St. Paul, The Beatle) said, "If I do not have charity, I am nothing." Have we dared to look for Christ among the poor, the needy, and the broken? As we give to the least, where will we see Christ in that moment?

Around Christmas I was feeling particularly overwhelmed by the commercialism of the season. In a little mountain town like this, there isn't anywhere to go to transcend this experience. The nativity scenes that scattered church lawns weren't doing it either. Where could I find Jesus? I found myself sitting in our town's soup kitchen. Canned Christmas music came over a small tape player. The tape was a little warbled from too much playing. I dropped off some groceries in the kitchen and sat in the dining room. It was decorated in Ala Tacky—tons of tinsel and flashing tree toppers that weren't on top of a tree. Wobbly patio tables heaved forward each time you slightly moved. There was a scattering of people in there—all with a different story as to why they were there. The Episcopal youth group had dropped off big urns of soup that were being dished out. Elderly women and teens were distributing food, smiles and Christmas carols to vacant-eyed people. Unshaven faces spooned soup to toothless mouths. In the background the tape cassette was skipping "Si-e-lent ni… Ho…Ni…Calm…Bright." But in my head my Christmas carol was "All You Need Is Love…"

Somewhere between the flashing tree toppers and the skipping tape cassette came Christ for a bowl of soup. I thought I saw Him sitting there…the mystery of Christmas visited me. Hum it… "All You Need Is Love…"

All You Need Is Love, Love, and More Love
Work Sheet

Theme: Charity and Service
Day One: Read full essay.
Day Two: Look up the "love passage" in 1st Corinthians. Write it here:

_____

_____

_____

_____

_____

_____

_____

Which aspects of love are you strong in?

_____

_____

_____

_____

_____

How can you use that in charity and service for others?

_____

_____

_____

_____

_____

Which aspects of love are you weak in?

_____

_____

_____

_____

How can you strengthen those in charity and service for others?

_____

_____

_____

_____

_____

Day Three: Give a biblical example of how Christ demonstrated each love aspect listed in 1st Corinthians:

_____

_____

_____

_____

_____

Demonstrate one of these love aspects today to someone.

Day Four: Today, find someone you do not know, someone that stretches your limits about who you would normally associate with. Talk to that person. As you talk to them, look for Christ hidden in that person. Write what happened:

_____

_____

_____

_____

_____

Day Five: Write a prayer asking the Lord to expand your heart for charity and service and to open doors for you to be active in that area:

_____

_____

_____

_____

Demonstrate another love aspect today to someone you do not know. Tell about it here:

_____

_____

_____

_____

Day Six: Demonstrate two other love aspects today to someone you do not know.

Tell about it here:

_____

_____

_____

_____

_____

Discuss the issue of charity and service with your partner or children. What were their thoughts?

_____

_____

_____

_____

Can you develop a family ministry of some sort; to volunteer once a month as a family somewhere?

_____

_____

_____

Day Seven: What did you learn this week?

_____

_____

_____

What do you need to do differently?

_____

_____

_____

What needs to change in your heart?

_____

_____

_____

What are you committed to doing about charity and service?

_____

_____

_____

(Note: Use extra sheets of paper, if required.)

Serenity, Simplicity and Solitude

Yeah, I know. This sounds like an oxymoron for boomers, X-ers and Y-ers. I hear ya.

We're techno junkies and noise addicts. We were raised on cartoons, concrete-vibrating rock and roll, and every kinda gadget that made a sound. We've blown our eardrums from concerts, our minds from God-knows-what, and our hearts from every get-well-quick self-help guru. We have lived so far away from serenity, simplicity and solitude that it's a totally foreign lifestyle.

Yeah, I know. Some of us, during our navel-gazing, "found ourselves" so we think we tapped into some karmic serenity there. We can all name those 70's self help books we read like brain-washed cult members. This was our serenity.

Yeah, I know. Some of us went off and joined the simplicity movement. We lived together in big houses, stopped shaving our armpits (why was this simple?), and drove Volkswagens with daisy decals until they were rust and tires. We avoided real jobs, lived off of Mother Earth and called this "simplifying." My dad called it "free loading."

This was our simplicity.

Yeah, I know. Then some of us sat around in a lotus position humming "MMMMM" with our fingertips slightly touching. We lit incense that gagged us and put on trippy music to meditate by. This was our solitude.

Yeah, I know. Now we're all grown up. We have substituted 70's self help books for 21st century self help books (Nurturing You're Anything and Everything Book, Your Inner Child Wants to Kill and Be on Day Time Talk TV Book). We've substituted our parents' B-O-R-I-N-G religion with its granny Sunday hats for our own anything-goes-reincarnation-Indian culture-past lives-mother earth-many paths lead to God-religion. Yeah, I know; we're all grown up now.

Yeah, I know. Now we're all grown up. We have substituted our living together in a big house for just owning a big house that puts us in mega-debt. We substituted not shaving our armpits for every type of cosmetic surgery imaginable. We are the Lipo-Anything Queens. We are financially in debt to the Society of Cosmetic Surgeons Association. We have substituted our Volkswagens with a Lexus and are in debt for that too. And we have substituted avoiding a real job with a workaholic schedule of 60-70 hours per week.

Yeah, I know; we're all grown up now.

Yeah, I know. Now we're all grown up. We have substituted meditating with hand-held pocket planners, beepers, cell phones, email, voice mail, faxes, and every other techno convenience to bring "solitude" and "more time" into our lives.

Yeah, I know; we're all grown up now!

It Irritates the Mind
Before It Calms It

I've always wanted a meditation water garden. The oriental ones did emanate a sort of serenity and I love the sound of water. I drove all over two counties looking for a pump and acquiring the rest of the goodies to create my corner for calming the soul. We hauled, dug, planted, arranged, rearranged and plugged it in. My husband was waiting for a deeply spiritual moment. After all, a terra cotta St. Francis stood in the middle of the garden with a church behind him. It was a 12th century backdrop just waiting for a prayer. He plugged in the pump and water began to fall from the figurine into a small pool.

"Should it sound like that?" he asked with a scowl. "Like—pouring water; shouldn't it sound lighter, easier on the ears? This is making me feel really irritated by the sound." It sounded like the London Symphony to me!

As I sat listening to my little symphony I remembered having read something about Christian meditation..."it irritates the mind before it calms it." Those who have tried to still their minds for prayer find it very hard and irritating, which is why so few people practice being quiet as a spiritual discipline. Our souls seem so opposed to soothing that anything that attempts to do so is met with irritation; whether it be falling water, a bird chirping, internal silence or even, hearing The Word preached. Those elements that lead us into a possibility of calm do their work by first showing us how irritated we live our lives.

Background noise of a TV, Nintendo or radio is preferred over water, wind, birds or the reading of the Psalms. The fall in the Garden of Eden produced the first evidence of irritation when Adam was irritated by what Eve did, when they were irritated that they were naked and irritated they were banned from parts of the Garden. From then on, we seem to have migrated as a people toward sources of irritation until this state of mind now feels normal. Faced with a quiet retreat in the woods, our mind races and our nerves are on edge. When "city folk" check into our cabins these are the complaints we get: "How can you sleep with no noise?" "The crickets are too loud." One person turned in the kitchen wall clock because "it's so quiet here and all I can hear is the ticking…it's reminding me every second that my life is moving ahead; it's very irritating." "The quietness shows me how bored I am."

So I suspect my water garden **won't** be a big hit this summer at the cabins. Someone will find a way to unplug it and probably ditch the classical music cassettes too. My 130 pound Akita, Molly, loves the water garden. She lies above it on a deck that overlooks it. She won't budge from the spot. She looks serene and meditative as I walk by her. She's way smarter than most of us. She has no anxiety disorder or medication to go with it. She has no heart disease or ulcers. The garden did not have to irritate her before it calmed. That's left for us humans.

I suspect our fabulous pink and lavender sunsets may be too loud too…

It Irritates the Mind Before It Calms It
Work Sheet

Theme: Serenity, Simplicity and Solitude

Day One: Read full essay.

Day Two: Close your eyes. Sit quietly for five minutes. Notice what your mind does.

When you are done, write down what you remember your mind doing:

_____

_____

_____

_____

_____

_____

Close your eyes. Sit quietly for five minutes. Only think about Christ. When you are done, write down what you remember your mind doing:

_____

_____

_____

What is the number one negative thing that is occurring to you because you do not have enough quiet space?

_____

_____

_____

_____

Day Three: What did you learn from yesterday's exercise?

_____

_____

_____

What did you notice most about your mind?

_____

_____

_____

What irritates your mind most?

_____

_____

_____

Research five scriptures on your mind and list them here:

_____

_____

_____

_____

Repeat Day Two.

_____

_____

_____

_____

_____

_____

_____

Day Four: What did you learn from scripture regarding your mind?

_____

_____

_____

_____

How much TOTAL quietness do you get a day?

_____

_____

_____

Make a commitment to your accountability partner to experience
   twenty minutes a day, every day.
What is it in your life that causes your mind to never be still?

_____

_____

_____

Repeat Day Two.

_____

_____

_____

_____

_____

Day Five: Why do you think "stillness" is a spiritual discipline?

_____
_____
_____
_____

Why is it hard to do, and hard to commit to?

_____
_____
_____
_____

What are your previous life messages about stillness, quiet, solitude?

_____
_____
_____
_____

Write a prayer asking God to help you honor this commitment of stillness.
Repeat Day Two.

_____
_____
_____
_____
_____
_____
_____

Day Six: On the Internet, research ten health benefits of stillness, quiet, or solitude.
Stop and listen to your environment right now and write down everything you hear:

_____
_____
_____
_____

What can you change about your environment that will encourage
more quietness?

_____

_____

_____

Repeat Day Two.

_____

_____

_____

_____

Day Seven: What was Christ's approach to stillness, quiet or solitude?

_____

_____

_____

_____

Why?

_____

_____

What did He believe about this?

_____

_____

_____

Why shouldn't you believe it too?

_____

_____

_____

Repeat Day Two.

_____

_____

_____

_____

(Note: Use extra sheets of paper, if required.)

The Ministry of Presence

...the newsletter said. "The Ministry of Presence"...I said it out loud as I rolled it around in my heart. It felt familiar and distant at the same time. I saw it mentioned in John Michael Talbot's newsletter. He spoke of it reverently—as a gift we give others. But how many of us are ever "really present?" Wouldn't The Ministry of Presence actually require people to be mentally present—not talking about themselves, ruminating, sorting emotional laundry in their heads, or preparing what they will say back to you...but actually present, open and available? It was a wishful, refreshing thought that there might be a place for this type of ministry.

Isn't our whole life really about The Ministry of Presence? On the best of days, perhaps, this is what counseling is supposed to be. This is what pastoring, nursing, social work, marriage, parenting and friendship is to be. I realize it's the only real thing we can give anyone. Presence precedes love, friendship, anything of value in a relationship because anything healthy in a relationship will be built off of the presence.

Isn't that what Jesus really offered others? What was happening in the midst of a healing? The *ultimate presence* was so powerfully focused on one person that they were immediately healed. Jesus' presence to the adulterer or the woman at the well had such impact that it changed their lives. What about his searing presence during His crucifixion; He could still be focused enough on others to cry out for the Father to not condemn them as they killed Him? The Holy Spirit's presence is what we call out for in worship, what we kneel to invoke, what we wait on for anointing.

Today this struck me at my job. I was traveling out into the rural areas to make home visits to my patients. I began to see that my job really is just The Ministry of Presence. Mrs. Bunson wanted to tell me about her sister's funeral and how much she missed her. Mr. Potts wanted to show me the white squirrels in his back yard. Ms. Cotter wanted to take me out to her garden to show me how her lettuce was coming up. Ms. Whitaker wanted to share her sugar free pudding recipe with me. It brightened their day. They felt seen and alive and heard. Presence changed their day from the ordinary to the extraordinary. Hearing about the funeral, watching some squirrels, squatting down to see some lettuce and writing down a recipe made a difference.

Perhaps it is one of the best lessons Jesus demonstrated for us: Presence. But can we live this in our daily lives? Lauren, my daughter, puts her head in my door and tells me she helped the coroner load a dead body onto the gurney. It was her first time as a nursing assistant. She flops on my bed and says, "Miss Mae died and I lifted her legs onto the gurney. Her husband was there because they lived together in the nursing home. He cried and said, 'I love you Mae. I'm going to lay down in my bed now and try to go be with you.' Isn't that sad, Mom, just really, really sad?"

Presence—I say, "Yeah, it's sad. But I am glad you got to help her. Was it as bad as you thought it would be?" "No, it's not bad when you care about someone" she says.

Presence—I am quiet for a while. I think she'll make a great nurse. Presence precedes everything.

The Ministry of Presence
Work Sheet

Theme: Serenity, Simplicity and Solitude
Day One: Read full essay.
Day Two: What is your concept of The Ministry of Presence?

_____

_____

_____

_____

_____

How could someone demonstrate this to you so that you could experience it for yourself?

_____

_____

_____

Go speak to someone right now; practice being open and focused on what they are saying. Notice any difficulties you have remaining focused on them.
Write down what you noticed:

_____

_____

_____

_____

Day Three: What do you do most often when people are speaking to you?

_____

_____

_____

Name all the ways you are not present when people speak to you:

_____

_____

_____

Describe Christ's gift of Presence to us:

_____

_____

Write a prayer asking for God to help you be more present to others:

_____

_____

_____

_____

Repeat Day Two.

_____

_____

_____

_____

_____

Day Four: Begin your day vowing to be more Present to at least one
person today.

Notice how many opportunities are available for you to give the gift of
Presence to people today. Now describe all those opportunities:

_____

_____

_____

_____

How many opportunities did you truly engage in with Presence?

_____

_____

_____

_____

Repeat Day Two.

_____

_____

_____

_____

_____

Day Five: Research scripture and show five examples of someone being Present to others:

_____

_____

_____

_____

What is your social conditioning regarding Presence, i.e., what have
    you been taught by culture about this?

_____

_____

_____

_____

Name a person that currently gives you the gift of Presence:

_____

_____

_____

_____

Why does this feel special?

_____

_____

_____

_____

Repeat Day Two.

_____

_____

_____

_____

_____

_____

Day Six: Name a person who is never Present.

_____

_____

_____

Why do you think that is?

_____

_____

_____

_____

How are they like you?

_____

_____

How does it make you feel?

_____

_____

How have you noticed it makes others feel?

_____

_____

Repeat Day Two.

_____

_____

_____

_____

Day Seven: Be Present to seven people today. This does not mean "doing" something for them. It means giving them your own Presence. Record the events:

_____

_____

How does not being Present affect your life, serenity, simplicity and solitude?

_____

_____

What is your commitment to this spiritual discipline going to be?

_____

_____

(Note: Use extra sheets of paper, if required.)

Doing "the V"
(The Boomer's version of vacation)

It is Memorial Day weekend. As a means of prayer, Ken and I drove up to the Blue Ridge Parkway to view God from the top-down. We always get a proportional sense of ourselves that way. We sat at Cherry Cove this morning, elevation 4,327 feet. It was a huge expanse where at least five mountain ranges could be seen. We sat in the car sort of awe struck. It takes a while for the sense of how beautiful it is, how big God is, and how insignificant we are to sink in, at least for us.

Cherry Cove Overlook was busy this morning. We saw Kentucky, a couple of Florida's, two Mississippi's, three Virginias and five South Carolinas whip into Cherry Cove Overlook. Not being blown over by the beauty, they simply leaned out the window, shot a picture with an instamatic and spun out to rush to the next overlook to repeat this "doing vacation" thing. I was stunned into sobriety and sadness.

Ken and I had been talking about why our cabin rentals were down this year. It was becoming clearer as we sat there. We talked about how vacationers are changing and how what they want keeps growing and turning into this whole adventure/experience instead of a time of good old fashion "R & R." At the last Chamber of Commerce meeting, they discussed the "new emerging vacationer" who wants instant experiences in three days.

Here was drive-by vacation at its best. One drives, the other says "oooh, ahhh, it's beautiful" and snaps a picture. One paddles the canoe; the other runs the video camera. In three days they have recorded most of western North Carolina. They haven't seen anything, but they have captured it on one type of film or the other. One of God's true Master Pieces, The Blue Ridge Mountains, was "done" in drive-by appreciation. It's no wonder us Boomer's approach our relationship with God in a similar fashion. On Sundays we show up—one drives the other prays. One says "oooh, ahhh," the other one kneels. It's church, then to breakfast, then to Home Depot, then to work in the yard, then to a cook out and home at last, to do laundry. There, whew, Sunday is "done."

New Vacationer Profile:

Average length of vacation days: 3

Average % of people who also bring work on vacation: 72%

Number of things they want to do on 3-day vacation: 5+

Average % of people who feel rested after vacation: **Why ask?**

Telling us to "stop and smell the roses" hasn't worked yet. Maybe "stop and see the view" will.

Doing "the V"
Work Sheet

Theme: Serenity, Simplicity and Solitude

Day One: Read full essay.

Day Two: Describe a normal vacation for you:

_____

_____

_____

_____

Describe your last vacation:

_____

_____

_____

Describe a vacation of your childhood:

_____

_____

_____

What do you notice?

_____

_____

_____

_____

Day Three: What was Christ's position on true "rest?"

_____

_____

_____

Research five scriptures on rest and list them here:

_____

_____

_____

_____

_____

What did you notice?

_____

_____

_____

_____

What is your view on R&R?

_____

_____

_____

_____

What is culture's message about R&R?

_____

_____

_____

Day Four: How much "down" time do you have a week? (P. S. This
means doing nothing…yes, nothing.)

_____

_____

_____

What is your physical health like?

_____

_____

_____

How much of the negative is stress related?

_____

_____

_____

Do vacations help your stress level?

_____

_____

_____

Why?

_____

_____

_____

Day Five: This week, schedule one day off in the near future (this month).
Do not "plan" this day off to the hilt. Leave it blank.
When the day comes, still leave it blank.
Live it blank.
Write what you think this will be like and what it makes you feel like just thinking about it:

_____

_____

_____

_____

Day Six: Discuss with your accountability partner how to incorporate more rest time for yourself.
Next vacation, **do nothing.** Plan a vacation that does not "go somewhere to see something". It is a vacation to lie around and read books.
Begin discussing this type of vacation with whom you will spend it.

What are their reactions?

_____

_____

_____

_____

Day Seven: How else do you "do life" in a drive-by fashion?

_____

_____

_____

_____

What proactive thing can you do to stop this insanity?

_____

_____

_____

_____

Mark the next four Sundays on your calendar as "**Do Nothing Days.**" and then really do it (no laundry, no lawn mowing). Go mark your calendar now.

Write a letter to The American Work Ethic and tell it you are temporarily off duty.

_____

_____

_____

_____

_____

_____

_____

_____

_____

_____

(Note: Use extra sheets of paper, if required.)

"Silence Is..."

"...the beginning of wisdom," as told to us by Thomas Merton, a Trappist Monk. Trappists take a vow of silence, although it isn't completely silent, as they do sing. They just learned to shut up. One of the first books I read of his was *The Silent Life*. I guess I read it because I couldn't comprehend the point of it all. Ken and I both talk too much. I talk too much in giving advice and analyzing every situation to death. Ken talks too much in telling people every tiny detail of his life when they are clearly disinterested. Ken can talk for hours about the weather and I can talk for days about "10 Ways to Change Your Life in 10 Seconds." We have found ourselves to be very obnoxious.

Technology fuels this universal message that we need to constantly "communicate" and "be in touch" at least, externally. We have cell phones, home phones, call waiting, voice mail, email, pagers, fax, internet, computers, TVs, radios, books on tape, videos. We have countless ways to externally expel our words in a classical display of "verbal bulimia." Ironically, we have never been more "out of touch." We have every sort of gadget to put our words "out there." Too bad we don't have all these gadgets to keep our words in us. It is noteworthy that technology isn't interested in developing equipment that would take our communication and turn it back in to us. What would that be like? Who would buy it other than schizophrenics whom would welcome a voice to talk to, even if it's their own? We actually do already have this "gadget." The gadget of communication and being in touch internally is prayer and silence. Technology cannot mass-produce that.

We got to see how hard being silent is. One night we were having two-thirds of a family meeting. We were all there, but Lauren was mad at Ken for something he "said" and asked that he just "listen" to her and I work out a problem. Ken said he would. Lauren bet he could not sit through it without talking. He was sure he could. As we began talking, Lauren verbalized the renowned teen-age logic that makes parents' brains turn inside out and fry inside their heads. It was bizarre, of course it made no sense, and it was totally irrelevant to what we were trying to discuss. (But such is the conversation of teens!) Ken blurted something out about her irrational dialogue. Lauren reminded him he promised not to talk. He squirmed and tried to muster up self-control. Lauren rambled on about more incongruent things and again Ken blurted something out. This continued for most of the night until we all finally laughed and knew Ken couldn't be silent, not even for an hour.

It took me a long time to learn to be silent. In 1997 when I was separated from most of my family, silence was inevitable. It was the enemy that slowly became a friend. Merton talked about the silence and how some Monks had complete nervous breakdowns from it. It wasn't the silence that drove them mad; it was the non-silence of their interior world. Silence is never really silence. When we shut up externally, our interior world cranks up the volume. Our external communication drowns out the internal, which is what we are avoiding.

Merton spoke of what silence accomplishes—the stripping a way of our illusionary self until we see our real self, which according to the Apostle Paul is our "wretch or worm" self. This was the madness that some of the Monks arrived at. I think they thought they would only arrive at seeing God's Glory in their silence, but the arrival there was first through the wilderness, the exile of self, and then the ascent to God's Glory. Some of the Monks got lost in the wilderness of their own selves where reality and insight was stark. The desert experience is full of darkness that yells out our own inadequacies or tempts us in ways Jesus was tempted. Jesus' silence in the wilderness was met with the demands we all face in silence. He handled it better than we do, but He must have known that "silence is the beginning of wisdom" as silence was part of His own discipline. The insight that is spoken of here is the insight into our own nature, and then Christ's nature, thus God's nature. Silence doesn't dump us in the lap of God's nature until we have first passed through the "Sheol" of our selves. Isn't that exactly what we don't want? What obvious power silence has.

My spiritual growth really didn't take off until I was "cast into silence." When Ken and I would vacation here in North Carolina, what I looked forward to most was the silence… the absence of whining clients, car stereos that vibrated the pavement, the phone, Nintendo noises. I'd say to Ken, "Shhh, listen!" And he'd say, "What? I don't hear anything." My life began to change each year I spent in North Carolina at the cottages. There was a beautiful stretch of road where huge Hemlocks and Pines grew together over the road forming a canopy, thick with fragrant pine needles. It was the most beautiful sanctuary I have ever been in. I've walked that path for years now, silent, listening, and often praying for our lives. It is a path that God faithfully spoke to me on, year after year, as I sat with my back against a 100-year-old Hemlock tree, silent.

It was this same stretch of road that God called me to one October when I didn't know if I could go on, when I didn't know what would happen to our family life. It was on this road, saturated with the prayers of years past, that spiritual warfare of sorts was enacted. That stretch of road had taught me the power of silence, the voice of God in silence, and it was from these years of silence on that path that I was drawn to wage the battle for my family. It is holy ground—with the presence of God thick like the fragrance of the forest. The silence that path brought changed me over the years; slowly peeling away layers of self, until God loomed large like the Hemlocks. God spoke in the pauses, the commas of silence, His work of redemption pregnant in the passages of quiet time—alone, and yet never alone. There is a fullness in silence, swelling until it spills over into reality and then a burst of praise. In this time of cheap imitations, there is not one for silence. It stands immortalized as a great truth from creation until eternity.

"Silence Is..."
Work Sheet

Theme: Serenity, Simplicity and Solitude

Day One: Read full essay.

Day Two: Why do you talk too much?

_____

_____

What do you mostly talk about?

_____

_____

_____

Why?

_____

_____

_____

Listen to yourself all day, as if you were an outsider listening to you. What did you notice?

_____

_____

_____

Day Three: Find thirty minutes today and be totally silent. (No radio, TV, or self-induced back ground noise).

Write down what you notice internally and externally:

_____

_____

Day Four: Repeat Day Three.

_____

_____

_____

Day Five: Research seven scriptures on silence. Write them here:

_____

_____

_____

What did you notice?

_____

_____

What does Christ say about silence?

_____

_____

_____

Repeat Day Three.

_____

_____

_____

Day Six: Why is silence hard?

_____

_____

_____

Discuss this with your accountability partner.
Would you be willing to try an eight-hour silence? Discuss it with your
accountability partner and plan it.
What are the benefits of silence that you have noticed?

_____

_____

_____

Repeat Day Three.

_____

_____

_____

Day Seven: Increase your daily silence to one hour today.
Write a prayer asking God to teach you about silence.

_____

_____

_____

Share your silence experiences with someone you think will benefit
from it. (But keep it brief!)
(Note: Use extra sheets of paper, if required.)

Don't Be Unequally Yoked

T he scripture says to not be unequally yoked, therefore, there is no solution to this! We have to get divorced because we cannot be in a relationship together and disagree this way!" I say manipulatively. It is our weekly joke.

"I say Neil Diamond was the best song writer!" Ken says with a completely straight face.

"Oh my gosh! What bubble gum junk is that? You wouldn't know real music if it bit that big behind of yours" I tort. "Of course this is coming from someone that thinks The Bee Gees actually produced something other than voices that sounded like fingernails on a chalk board" I add.

Ken fires back, "The Bee Gees are great!" I am immediately sorry I said it, as he stretches on his tip toes to sing a Bee Gees song and hit those awful high notes that no man "in tact" can reach.

I marvel that I married a man who **liked** the Bee Gees and Neil Diamond. I mean he truly did. I never met someone who really liked them…and owned their records. I thought the same people who listened to Lawrence Welk probably bought those kinds of records. I am a Zepplin, Moody Blues, Leon Russell, Hendrix kinda girl. He is a Bee Gees, Diamond, Croce, Bread, Three Dog Night bubble-gum boy. Luckily in real life that isn't a problem. This unequal-ness merely affects our entertainment preferences.

But unequal-ness in other things can be problematic. Jesus didn't hang out with the Pharisees. Divinity and anal-ness were definitely not equally yoked. On the other hand, Jesus did hang out with prostitutes, tax collectors, and lepers. This is not a contradiction. Jesus hung out with those whose hearts were open like His. People, despite their current condition, were seeking truth and found hanging with Him was a cool and a restorational thing to do.

Jesus warned against pairing up with those who are not on the same page as us. Most of us co-dependents like to think that we will be just the influence someone needs to turn their life around. We go in for the rescue and get pulled under in the tidal wave. Jesus knows that we sometimes don't have the strength to save anyone but ourselves, which is why He says to seek out those that we are linked to in Him. It sure eliminates a lot of problems; to avoid those things that cannot naturally link with us.

I recently relearned this truth in a session I had with a therapist to discuss my own mounting depression. In the final analysis, it was someone else's dark spirituality and life outlook that was pulling me under. We aren't a good match. I'm a Christian; she is "other." I am this, she is that. I believe in reaping and sowing, she in karma and re-incarnation. There really isn't much we can line up under the column "agreed" and live happily ever after. I was surprised to be back learning this AGAIN. The spiritual thread runs throughout our lives and touches everything in our lives. If we aren't pointed in the same direction, we are pulling against each other.

"Grand Funk! You liked them didn't you?" He asks hopefully.

"Oh, please! Where were you when real music existed like the Stones and Jefferson Airplane? Were you still playing with GI Joes?" I accuse.

"Hey, I liked GI Joes. Don't say anything bad about them! What about the Eagles?" he says trying to compromise.

"Ok, ok, The Eagles! We will leave it at that. You are declared cool again. You liked the Eagles." I say trying to hit a middle ground. He smiles confidently. I turn to go into the bedroom and mumble under my breath, "yeah, but you played with GI Joes."

Don't Be Unequally Yoked
Work Sheet

Theme: Serenity, Simplicity and Solitude

Day One: Read full essay.

Day Two: Look up the scripture about being unequally yoked. Write it here:

_____

_____

_____

_____

_____

Research to see if there are any other scriptures about being with people that you are not linked to spiritually. Write them here:

_____

_____

_____

_____

Day Three: What did Christ have to say about this issue?

_____

_____

_____

Who comes to mind that you are "unequally yoked with?"

_____

_____

_____

How does it manifest itself in your relationship?

_____

_____

_____

How did you come to be together in the first place?

_____

_____

_____

Day Four: What scriptural guidelines should we use when determining relationships with others?

_____

_____

_____

_____

How can you avoid being unequally yoked in the future?

_____

_____

_____

_____

List five things you should look for in others to help you determine the kind of relationship or yoking that would develop.

_____

_____

_____

_____

Day Five: What is the difference between discerning being unequally yoked and judging another person?

_____

_____

_____

_____

How can you make sure you are not judging?

_____

_____

_____

How does this yoking affect your serenity?

_____

_____

_____

_____

Day Six: Write a prayer asking God to help you see what areas you are unequally yoked in and to help you develop discernment to not repeat this in the future:

_____

_____

_____

_____

Discuss this with your accountability partner.
How does this yoking affect your simplicity?

_____

_____

_____

Day Seven: How does this yoking affect your solitude?

_____

_____

_____

In the past, how did you choose whether or not to hang out with someone?

_____

_____

_____

How did that turn out?

_____

_____

_____

How can that be different today?

_____

_____

_____

Will it be?

_____

_____

_____

(Note: Use extra sheets of paper, if required.)

Epilogue

L adies and gentlemen, the "Magical Mystery Tour" is coming to our final destination. We are glad you were able to join us and we hope the Tour provided you with groovy insights, a few legal flashbacks, and some good ol' rock and roll. Of course, none of that matters if you haven't figured out how to apply it all to your life and your walk with God. To that end, we hope that you've had some time now to consider your "walk;" whether it was down "Penny Lane," through "Strawberry Fields," or up the "Stairway to Heaven." Everyone's walk is different.

We hope the Tour showed that "Rocky Raccoon" and *Leave It to Beaver* can help you figure out that whatever you lived through to get to the pew is relevant. Maybe the Tour showed you that Dr. Seuss and Kenny Rogers both let you know that disciples come in many packages and you are just as likely to be one as they were. The Tour, through *M*A*S*H** and George Carlin, hopefully pointed to understanding that The Body of Christ is a rowdy bunch—and you're one of them—so hop in! And that Janis Joplin is a good way of understanding about prosperity theology. The Tour by the way of *Lost in Space* is just as good a teaching about the Holy Spirit as I got in Bible College or you probably got from the pulpit. So don't be intimidated by those big theological words. The bus that went by Cat Stevens and Bob Dylan highlighted that they can preach redemption as good as any preacher if your ears are tuned in. The original "Magical Mystery Tour" that belonged to The Beatles—well they taught us everything didn't they? Before we knew about 1st Corinthians, there was The Beatles—saying all the same stuff...love, love, love.

What I hope you learned is that what you lived through in the 60's, 70's and 80's is all applicable to your spiritual life. You don't have to get cleaned up to look spiritual—at least, not in Jesus' way of looking at things. We are not the spiritual rejects of our day because we happened to have lived through the turbulence of the "wild eras." We can be the wise men, the sages, the spiritual masters and the desert Mamas & Papas of the church today! Our depth and life experiences are valuable. We have knowledge to contribute to our own and other's spiritual growth. We already know that the New Testament Book of Led Zepplin did not fail us! It's still with us so it's still usable if we glean and learn. We have to stop denying who we are, what we know, and how we came to know it.

So wander a little deeper in—sit a few pews closer to the front. You are in good company with some pew-dewlling radicals. Keep the faith and the journey!

If you enjoyed this book and would like to pass one on to someone else or if you're interested in another Tsaba House title, please check with your local bookstore, online bookseller, or use this form:

Name _____

Address _____

City _____ State_____ Zip _____

Please send me:

_____ copies of *The Moody Pews* at $15.99 $_____

_____ copies of *Streams of Mercy* at $15.99 $_____

_____ copies of *The Payload* at $15.99 $_____

_____ copies of *Your Rights to Riches* at $14.99 $_____

_____ copies of *The Parenting Business* at $15.99 $_____

California residents please add sales tax $_____

Shipping*: $4.00 for the first copy and $2.00
for each additional copy $_____

Total enclosed $_____

Send order to:

> Tsaba House
> 2252 12th Street
> Reedley, CA 93654

or visit our website at www.TsabaHouse.com
or call (toll free) 1-866-TSABA-HS (1-866-872-2247)

For more than 5 copies, please contact the publisher for multiple copy rates.

*International shipping costs extra. If shipping to a destination outside the United States, please contact the publisher for rates to your location.